LITTLE BOOK OF
VIDEO GAMES

Andrew O'Brien

LITTLE BOOK OF
VIDEO GAMES

First published in the UK in 2013

© Demand Media Limited 2013

www.demand-media.co.uk

Printed and bound in China

ISBN 978-1-909217-38-6

Contents

Chapter 1

The Birth of Video and Computer Games

To understand when and how video games were first conceived, you have to begin in the technological arms race of the Cold War. On February 14, 1946, exactly six months after Japan had surrendered and the Second World War finally came to an end, the University of Pennsylvania switched on the first programmable computer: the Electronic Numeric Integrator and Calculator (ENIAC for short).

The state of the art machine – labelled by the media as a "giant brain" – took three years to build and was a colossus of a machine, weighing 30 tons and taking up 63 metres of floor space. It had no screen or keyboard and instructions were fed in using punch cards. Despite its myriad limitations, a clear start had been made and this innovation acted as a catalyst for a renewed vigour to develop new computer technology.

Many renowned intellectuals had become fascinated by the potential for artificial intelligence and its status as the ultimate aim of computer research before and during the Second World War, foremost among them British mathematician Alan Turing and American computer expert Claude Shannon. Their theories would form the foundation of modern computing and both agreed that getting a computer to defeat a human at Chess would be a

significant step to realising their dream.

In 1947, Turing became the first person to write a computer Chess program, but his code was so advanced that none of the primitive computers that existed at the time had the capacity to run it. Sadly, he would never get the chance to attempt his ideas for computer Chess as he was arrested in 1952 and convicted of homosexuality. Two years later he took his own life.

Shannon and computer scientist Alex Berstein, perhaps spurred on by the tragic loss of Turing and his determination to pioneer computer technology, spent most of the 1950s investigating artificial intelligence by making computers play games. Many of the principles pioneered by Shannon and others would later be used by video game designers to create challenging computer-controlled opponents for game players. But while Chess remained the ultimate test, others brought simpler games to life.

In 1950, an Australian employee of computer company Ferranti, came to the rescue after his company were struggling to fulfil its promise to contribute to the two-year national event, the Festival of Britain's Exhibition of Science in London, which was to be launched in 1951.

John Bennett suggested creating a computer that could play the simple parlour game, Nim. Bennett got the idea from the Nimatrom, an electro-mechanical machine exhibited at the 1940 World's Fair in New York. His aim was not to entertain but to show off the ability of computers to do mathematics, and Nim was a prime example to achieve this goal.

The computer exhibit was named the Nimrod and by April 12, 1951 it was ready. Standing five feet tall and nine feet deep, the actual computer running the game accounted for no more than two per cent of its size. The bulk of the machine was due to the plethora of vacuum tubes used to display lights. The exhibit made its public debut on May 5, 1951 and boasted that the Nimrod was "faster than thought." The public was

won over but few showed interest in the science behind the machine, they just wanted to play.

After the Festival of Britain came to an end, the Nimrod went on display at the Berlin Industrial Show, where it received a similar response. But having impressed the public, Ferranti eventually dismantled the Nimrod and went back to work on more serious projects.

Another traditional game to make an early transition to computers was Noughts and Crosses. The game was recreated on the Electronic Delay Storage Automatic Calculator (EDSCA) at Cambridge University, built in 1949 by Professor Maurice Wilkes. The EDSAC was the first computer with memory that users could read, add or remove information from and was as much a landmark in computing as the ENIAC.

Meanwhile, over the Atlantic, Arthur Samuel was trying to recreate Checkers on an IBM machine. He wanted to create a game that could defeat a human player and he completed his first game in 1952 on an IBM 701 – the first

ABOVE IBM 701 console

commercial computer created by the company. By 1955 Samuel had developed a version that could learn from its mistakes and after it was shown on television the company's share leapt by 15 per cent.

At the same time as scientists were teaching computers to play board games, televisions were making their way into people's homes. In 1947, TV network Dumont became the first to try and explore the idea of allowing people to play games on their TV sets. Two Dumont employees – Estle Mann and

Thomas Goldsmith – came up with the Cathode-Ray Tube Amusement Device, which would allow people to fire missiles at a target stuck onto the screen by the player. However, the device was never turned into a commercial product.

A few years later, TV engineer Ralph Baer tried something similar. In 1951, Baer and some of his colleagues at military contractors Loral Electronics were asked to build a television set from scratch. While he was attempting this he came up with the idea of building a

BELOW Tennis for Two controller

game into the television set. He quickly cast it aside but a seed had been sown.

By 1958, the concept of a video game was still elusive, but it would come one step closer to fruition, courtesy of William Higinbotham. Higinbotham had worked on the Manhattan Project and after the war he became head of the instrumentation division at the Brookhaven National Laboratory, a US government research facility in New York.

Every year, Brookhaven opened its doors to the public to show off its work and in 1958, Higinbotham decided to showcase a more engaging attraction, and Tennis for Two was born.

The game was operated by two large, box-shaped controllers, which allowed players to move their racquets using a dial and whack the ball by pressing a button – it proved to be a massive hit. The game was so popular it appeared for a second time the following year. However, it was dismantled the following year and Higinbotham returned to his efforts to stop nuclear proliferation.

His idea, though popular and engaging,

was the last example in a decade of false starts for the video game. Almost as soon as anybody began to explore the idea of a video game they became convinced it was a waste of time and walked away.

Spacewar!

However, by the dawn of the next decade, the idea that computers should only be used to serious endeavour was about to be challenged by a group of bright computing students from the Tech Model Railroad Club based at the Massachusetts Institute of Technology (MIT).

Many of the club's members shared a love of computing and sci-fi books, especially the work of E.E. Smith. His Lensman and Skylark series of books, written in the 1920s and 1930s, helped to define the space opera genre of science fiction and member of the club, particularly Steve Russell lapped up his escapist tales. As a result, the club members wanted to do the opposite of what had been tried before: to create something that seemed like a fun idea regardless of its practical value.

In late 1961, they got the chance to try and follow through on this idea, when the Digital Equipment Corporation (DEC) gave MIT its latest computer: the PDP-1. With the cutting edge technol-

ABOVE A PDP-1 computer running Spacewar

THE BIRTH OF VIDEO AND COMPUTER GAMES

BELOW The "brown box" prototype of the Magnavox Odyssey autographed by creator Ralph Baer

ogy of the PDP-1 at their disposal, the members decided to create a two-player spaceship duelling game. Spacewar! had been born. However, the game needed some serious improvement and modifications were needed, but by spring 1962 it was finally finished.

Soon word spread beyond the walls of MIT to the extent that DEC began using the game to demonstrate the PDP-!'s potential to customer. The game was thriving and growing in popularity, but it was also severely restricted by the technology needed to run it.

Meanwhile, the idea that Ralph Baer had had back in 1951 was about to come to fruition. Baer had written a proposal setting out his ideas for a game-playing device that would plug into a TV set. He used his position at the head of a large division within the military contracting company he worked, Sanders, to start work on his idea in secret.

Alongside two Bills – Harrison and Rusch – Baer came up with a working machine in 1967 and a host of game ideas, including a game of Ping-Pong, where players controlled bats at either side of the screen to deflect a ball that bounced around the screen.

Baer demonstrated his creation – now called the Brown Box – to the company's executive board, including company founder Royden Sanders. It received a positive response and by the end of the year the Brown Box was nearing completion.

ABOVE Ralph Baer with George W. Bush

However, despite attracting attention from a cable TV company, Sander's position as a military contractor meant it could just start making the Brown Box. The hope was that the cable company would buy the rights to produce it, but talks to do so fell through and Baer's toy was left on the shelf.

So yet again, video games in the shape of Spacewar! and video game equipment such as the Brown Box had come close to hitting the big time but had fallen short of becoming widespread. However, the creative force that video gaming needed to finally realise its potential was about to come to the fore.

Nolan Bushnell and the birth of Atari

Bushnell had discovered Spacewar! whilst studying at the University of Utah and a love affair with the game soon begun. He the bold decision to build a new version of the game, one that would capture the attention of the whole country. He teamed up with Ted Dabney, a fellow engineer at the Ampex Corporation, to try and design his coin-operated machine on paper.

Using the Data General Nova computer, which would boast four screens and four they set about realising their dream. But their first attempts stalled as the computer was simply too slow, and by 1970, Bushnell thought the project was doomed to failure.

But then he had his eureka moment, to get rid of the computer and do it all in hardware. From that point the project gathered momentum. Bit by bit Dabney and Bushnell created dedicated circuits to perform each of the functions they originally hoped the DGN would handle.

BELOW Nova 840

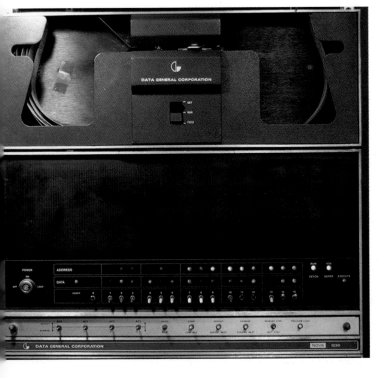

This process saw them overcome the technological obstacles they faced, plus it made the machine cheaper to build.

It also forced a rethink of the game itself. Now, players controlled one spaceship that had to shoot down two flying saucers controlled by the hardware. In short, it was no longer Spacewar!

By the summer of 1971 the game was nearly finished and its creators began to wonder who they could sell the game to. Of all things, it was a trip to the dentist that solved the problem. After telling his dentist of his plans, his dentist advised him to talk to one of his patients, a salesman at Nutting Associates. Bushnell simply called him up and negotiated a deal.

So, in August 1971, Bushnell left Ampex for Nutting Associates to complete work on the game he believed would transform the amusements business.

By now, the name of the game had changed to Computer Space. However, it soon became apparent to Bushnell that he wasn't the only one working on a major contender for the first ever commercially successful video game.

Fellow Spacewar! fans Bill Pitts and Hugh Tuck where working on their own version of the game, and when Bushnell

LEFT Nutting Computer Space - Blue

discovered their plans he invited them to Nutting's head office in California. Pitts thought Bushnell technology was excellent but believed that he and Tuck had the better game. Bushnell, on the other hand, concluded that he would learn nothing from the pair and that his plans were far from under threat.

And so only a few weeks later in September 1971, Pitts and Tuck's game, Galaxy Game, the first coin-operated

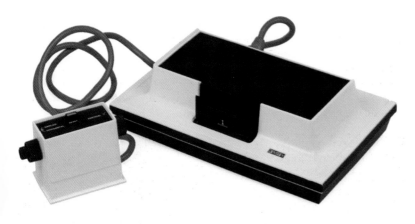

LEFT Magnavox
Odyssey Console

game in video game history, made its debut. It attracted crowds of people immediately. However, the amount that the pair spent building a second version meant that Pitts and Tuck couldn't justify the cost and soon they had to give up.

Bushnell wouldn't make the same mistake of underestimating the business element involved in making his dream succeed. In November 1971, the first Computer Space machine was installed at the Dutch Goose bar near the Stanford University campus and to Bushnell's delight the bar's clientele

seemed to like the game. However, people in the arcade business were confused by the game, and as time went by the attention the game received from Stanford's students also waned.

For Bushnell, the game had done well enough. His experience in creating the game at Nutting Associates had also inspired him to form his own business and with that Bushnell and Dabney formed Syzygy Engineering. Their company would focus on the solitary goal of delivering on Bushnell's claim that video games would replace pinball as the focus of arcade customers.

THE BIRTH OF VIDEO AND COMPUTER GAMES

At the same time as Bushnell and Dabney were moving on to their next step, Ralph Baer's Brown Box had seen renewed efforts to find a licensee prove successful. The Brown Box's three creators – Baer, Harrison and Rusch – had demonstrated their work to the television manufacturer Magnavox and they were convinced the Brown Box had a future. In January 1971, a preliminary deal was signed to turn the Brown

BELOW Atari 2600
Wood 4Sw Set

Box into a marketable product. The only thing they wanted to change was the name and so they settled on the Odyssey.

The Odyssey would be sold with 12 games, which included the Ping-Pong game developed back in 1967. The world's first games console was due to launch in August 1972 and only be available in Magnavox dealerships. On May 24, 1972, the company put the console on display at the Airport Marina in Burlingame, near San Francisco.

One of the people who decided to check out what all the fuss was about was Nolan Bushnell. By now, Bushnell and Dabney were busy creating video games for Chicago-based pinball behemoth Bally Midway. One of Bushnell's ideas was to create a successful driving game for the company and after seeing the Odyssey and its Ping-Pong game he was far from concerned that he faced stiff competition for the attention of the game-playing audience.

However, while they were working hard to creating the game, Bushnell and Dabney discovered that another company already had the Syzygy name. Using his favourite game – the Japanese board game Go – for inspiration, he suggested a term from the game that was similar to "check" in Chess. The term was Atari, and on June 27, 1972, Atari Incorporated was born.

All that video gaming now needed was a game to grab the attention of the masses and to help sell the potential of this new form of entertainment. The solution to this would make its first significant step on the same day Atari was born.

While he was toasting the birth of his new business venture, Bushnell was also busy hiring a young engineer called Al Alcorn, who Bushnell decided needed some basic video game technology training. And so, Bushnell gave Alcorn the unenviable task of creating a clever ping-pong game based on the game he had played on the Odyssey only a few weeks previously.

He described Ping-Pong to Alcorn and even though he knew the game would be too simplistic to become popular, he thought it would prove to be a good starting point for Alcorn.

However, Bushnell hadn't reckoned on Alcorn throwing himself into the project with the goal of changing his mind about the game. What happened next was to prove to be the birth of video gaming and usher in a restructuring of the entire amusements business, putting in place the foundations for the gigantic industry we know today.

LEFT Al Alcorn

Chapter 2

Pong – The Game That Started it All

Two circular dials control a pair of featureless white paddles, sliding up and down either side of a deep black monitor. A white dot – a ball without enough pixels to be an actual ball, more square than spherical – bleeps and bounces between the two. From bars to doctors' waiting rooms to unlicensed mini-cab operations, Atari's Pong, for many, was the First Coming: Year Zero.

The mechanics that Alcorn delivered based on Bushnell's specific brief proved addictive in their basic form and, importantly, easier to understand than anything they, or the general public, had ever seen. He improved the game by making the ball bounce

off the player's bats at different angles depending on which part of the bat it hit. He also added scores and basic sound effects. The result had just one instruction: "Avoid missing ball for high score".

These minor improvements did not drastically change the game but were enough to make Bushnell and Dabney change their plans. They were convinced this game could be the one to hit

the big time, the only change Bushnell made was with the name. He decided on Pong.

Bally Midway was not sold on the new two-player game but the game's testing at Andy Capp's Tavern in Sunnydale, California was a resounding success. It was so popular that the game had stopped working due to the amount of coins in the machine, causing it to seize up. Atari knew it had a hit

ABOVE LEFT
Nolan Bushnell

ABOVE RIGHT Tele
Games Atari Pong

PONG – THE GAME THAT STARTED IT ALL

on its hands and when Bally Midway rejected the game, the company decided to gamble everything on its first run of Pong machines.

Word of mouth about the game had spread throughout the arcade business and distributors all over the country were desperate for the machines. With funding secured, Atari needed an

BELOW APF TV Fun pong console. Model with two paddle in the body of the console

instantly available workforce to start creating a production line of machines.

With this in place, Pong machines started to take the US by storm and the idea of the video game was now one that was apparent to the masses. Before long it had proven so successful that the game went global. Meanwhile, desperate to cash in on this new craze, several amusement machine manufacturers started to rapidly produce their own versions of the game.

Meanwhile, Atari came to an agreement with Magnavox after both Baer and Magnavox had become aware of Bushnell's plans to make a home version. After documents, including a signed guest book that proved Bushnell had played Baer's Ping-Pong before Pong was released, were shown to a court, Bushnell decided it would be better to come to an agreement that suited both sides.

So, Magnavox came to an agreement with Atari that instead of suing the nascent company for infringing Ralph Baer's patents, it would give Atari the rights for a one-off fee of $700,000,

PIN CONFIGURATION
28 LEAD DUAL IN LINE

Top View

Left pins	#	#	Right pins
Horizontal Motion Select Input	1	28	Composite Picture Data
Vss (Ground)	2	27	Hit Input
Sound Output	3	26	Shot Input
Vcc	4	25	Reset Input
Ball Angles	5	24	Field Output
White/Black Bat Select	6	23	Practice
Ball Speed	7	22	Squash
Manual Serve	8	21	Soccer
Right Player Output	9	20	Tennis
Left Player Output	10	19	Rifle Game 2
Right Bat Vertical Input	11	18	Rifle Game 1
Left Bat Vertical Input	12	17	Clock Input
Bat Size	13	16	Sync Output
Right Bat Horizontal Input	14	15	Left Bat Horizontal Input

ABOVE AY-3-8550 chip pinout

leaving Magnavox free to sue others.

Pong also helped Magnavox sell its Odyssey console and by 1974, mainly on the back of its Ping-Pong game, around 200,000 had been sold.

The game's popularity sent shockwaves through the industry and in less than six months Atari had gone from an unknown start-up company to the leaders of an arcade revolution. And its effect on the game-playing public saw video games transform the way television was seen. No longer was the television simply to be used for viewing pleasure, now the viewer could take control.

Pinball tables and electro-mechanical games were becoming to be regarded as things of the past as video games were embraced and as a result Atari knew that they couldn't stand still: they needed to expand its range of games.

But following the success of Pong would prove to be an onerous task for Bushnell

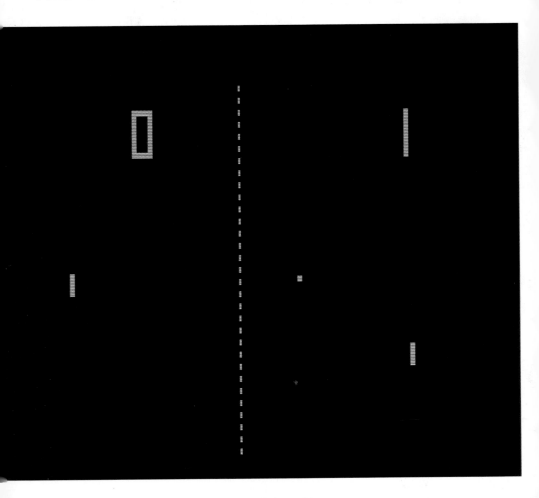

and his contemporaries, and the next game to capture the attention would not arrive for another six years, when the arrival of Space Invaders finally led to gaming's true global takeover from Taito's Tokyo HQ.

And how is Pong regarded in today's sophisticated gaming industry? As well as being the forerunner to every two-player video game based on a single screen in existence, Pong has inspired a plethora of gaming classics. Metal Gear Solid publisher Konami traded the jukebox business for arcades after seeing the game's success, while Nintendo's version of the game lifted the company out of its financially bar-ren years.

Nintendo's Wii console is the most recent high-profile gaming success to reference Bushnell and Alcorn's magic. The con-sole's Wii Sports – a 3D take on Bushnell's mantra of family-unifying gaming

– successfully made gaming socially acceptable once more.

Having celebrated its fortieth birthday in 2012, Pong's influence has perme-ated popular culture far and wide. From Saturday Night Live sketches to a groundbreaking television commercial featuring American tennis star Andy Roddick that mimics the game's simple appeal, Pong is shorthand for retro cool.

LEFT Pong graphics

BELOW Screenshot of Interton, a Pong like game

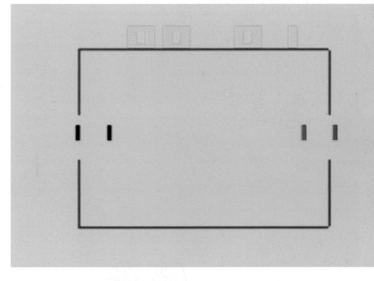

Chapter 3

The Golden Age of Video Arcade Games

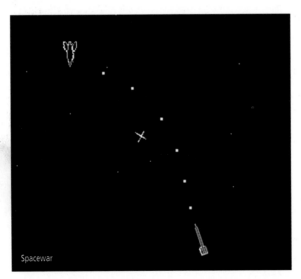

Spacewar

The Golden Age is defined as the peak era of arcade video game popularity and technological innovation. Before Ralph Baer and Nolan Bushnell brought these systems into people's homes and before pizza parlours started to become omnipresent, these systems were still abstract concepts.

However, it is during this era that video games began to truly make their mark on society and culture, and although there is no consensus as to its exact time period, most sources place it as starting in the late 1970s and lasting to the mid-1980s.

During the late 1970s, video arcade game

technology had become sophisticated enough to offer good-quality graphics and sounds, but it was still fairly basic. Realistic images and full-motion video were not yet available, and only a few games used spoken voice. As a result, games relied solely on simple and fun gameplay to entice an audience.

This emphasis on the gameplay is why many of these games continue to be enjoyed today despite their technology being vastly outdated by modern computing technology.

ABOVE Nolan Bushnell at the Game Developers Conference Online 2011 and (inset) posing with Chuck E. Cheese after founding the outlet in 1977 where kids could eat pizza and play video games

The Rise of the Fallen Industry –
Space Invaders & Pac-Man

By 1977 the industry was in the doldrums. But then came the arrival of two games that both revolutionised and kick-started the modern video game industry: first Space Invaders and then Pac-Man.

BELOW Space Invaders

Space Invaders had originally been invented as a test used for evaluating computer programmers, but someone decided to convert the test into a video game to be distributed in Japan by Taito.

In the game, players moved a laser turret from side to side along the bottom of the screen, instead of controlling familiar objects. Aliens marched horizontally in a rectangular formation eight columns long and five rows deep and advanced toward the bottom of the screen. Players lost if the invading army reached the bottom or they lost all of their turrets.

To defend against the invaders, players had to shoot at the aliens with their laser turrets while avoiding missiles. Destroying an entire wave of aliens earned 990 points. Extra points could be earned by shooting flying saucers that flew across the top of the screen at 25-second intervals.

There was no way to beat Space Invaders as the aliens kept on coming until either the player gave up or was killed. The best you could hope for was to post the highest score of the day at the top of the screen, which meant it became a matter of personal pride for each player.

However, players' pulses would quicken along with the music as the aliens came closer, while blasting the flying saucer was as satisfying in its day as a Call of Duty or Medal of Honor kill shot would be nowadays.

The game's release came just as ground-breaking blockbuster Star Wars was hitting Japanese cinemas – and its timing could not have been better. Space Invaders was to become a phenomenon. In fact, it was so successful that it triggered a national shortage of ¥10 coins as children queued up to slot money into the new machines and the Japanese mint had to triple production of the coin.

Space Invaders wasn't the first ever arcade game, but it was the first to capture Japan's imagination, as dedicated arcades called "Invader Houses" sprang up all over the country. For more than a decade Japanese arcades were dominated by shooting games.

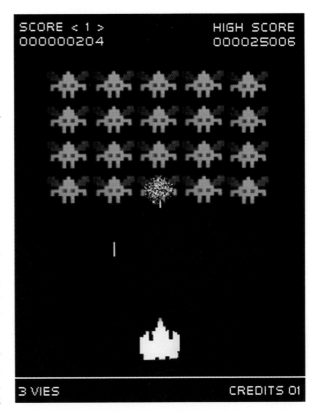

BELOW Spave Invaders style game

THE GOLDEN AGE OF VIDEO ARCADE GAMES

and the response was a resoundingly positive one.

Midway distributed the game in the country in 1978 and it proved a massive success straightaway. In fact, the orders poured in so quickly that the company became backlogged. Within a year, Midway sold more than 60,000 Space Invaders machines in the US

By 1979, Space Invaders's success had cemented the game's status as the catalyst for the renaissance for the video game industry. The game also inspired several copycat classics, such as Asteroids, Galaxian and Galaga.

This was also the year that saw the advent of vector graphics technology, which in turn spawned many of the popular early arcade games, including Atari classic Defender, often cited as one of the toughest games in arcade history.

ABOVE Ed Logg standing next to a very rare "Gold Asteroids" cabinet at Atari. Photo taken Spring 1999 at Atari Games in Milpitas, California

Just over twelve months later, the game arrived in America. However, even after the game's success in Japan, Taito executives felt that the game's theme of defending space stations from alien attack was too different from other games to appeal to American audiences. A secret testing location in Colorado was set up to see if the game would prove enticing to the American public

With the enormous success of these early games, dozens of developers jumped into the development and manufacturing of video arcade games – and one game in particular sent the industry into the stratosphere.

LITTLE BOOK OF **VIDEO GAMES**

Pac-Man

Launched in 1981, Pac-Man was the invention of Namco's Toru Iwatani and would become the best-selling coin-operated game in history. Iwatani, a young pinball enthusiast, had decided to build a game around the Japanese word taberu, which means "to eat." The first thing he produced was the eponymous character, which was a simple yellow circle with a wedge cut away for a mouth, an idea that came to him when Iwatani was having pizza for lunch.

The final game was exceptionally simple. Players had to guide Pac-Man around a maze of dots, closely followed by four ghosts who would seep through and try and catch Pac-Man. The player lost if the ghosts caught Pac-Man before he cleared all of the dots.

Once the game hit the arcades it quickly overshadowed all of the year's other releases, especially the hotly tipped Rally-X. In the game's debut year more than 100,000 Pac-Man machines were made and sold around the world, and before long it had become a phenomenon, with Pac-Man appearing on the cover of Time, inspiring a hit song and translating into a popular Saturday morning cartoons show.

The video game industry changed in the wake of Pac-Man's success. With the industry now extremely lucrative, arcades grew to be as common as convenience stores, with some hotels even replacing gift shops with arcades. Plus,

BELOW A girl enjoying playing Pac Man

BELOW Super Pac-Man - Woody's Diner - Sunset Beach, CA

the game's influence had seen gaming's most popular theme change from shooting games to mazes.

Sadly for the game's creator, the huge financial spoils of Pac-Man's success didn't exactly reach his pocket. Japanese employers seldom award big bonuses to employees for performing the work they were hired to do. Eventually, Iwatani was promoted to manager of research and development as a token of respect.

However, it was clear to all that video games had now entered an unforeseen period of success. Prior to this Golden Age, pinball machines were more popular than video games, but now the lure of the arcade hall and the dream of setting high scores and becoming the talk of the town were too great for players everywhere.

Arcade's Biggest Year

In 1981, Illinois teenager Steve Juraszek scored 15,963,100 points in a 16-hour game of Defender, setting a new world record and becoming an instant celebrity. However, there was a downside to his achievement as Jurascek began his record-breaking feat during school hours and the connection between video games and truancy was a stark one.

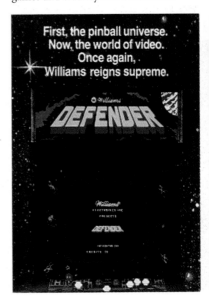

Disputes began, especially in small towns, about pushing for laws to monitor the operation of video game arcades. Other countries also struggled with the growth of video games.

A Time story reported that Americans had dropped 20 billion quarters into video games in 1981 and that the industry earned twice as much money as all Nevada casinos combined. Everywhere you looked across the US you would encounter arcades, with more than 1.5 million arcade machines in operation in the country.

However, the arcade industry's run of immense success would soon start to unravel and fade as quickly as it had risen.

Decline of arcades

The video game industry began its decline in mid 1982. The industry didn't crash, it simply stopped growing. With interest in arcade video games waning,

LEFT An original Defender promotional flyer

BELOW A rather dusty control panel of the arcade game Defender signals the decline

large new arcades attracted too few customers to meet expenses, becoming the first casualties of the shake-up.

And as they started to disappear, smaller ones received enough business to survive and for a while the industry seemed to correct itself. Many arcade owners purchased new equipment and tried to hang on until business picked up again.

Despite the release of some of the most memorable games in video game history, the industry began to fade and the public's love affair with the coin-operated video game began a steady decline that would last for many years.

However, arcade games experienced a brief resurgence in the early-to-mid-1990s with game such as Street Fighter II, Mortal Kombat, Virtua Racing and NBA Jam. But with the advent of 16-bit and 32-bit consoles, home video games began to approach, and even exceed, the level of graphics seen in arcade games, and increasing numbers of players would wait for popular arcade games to be ported to consoles.

This trend increased with the introduction of more realistic equipment to enhance computer and console game systems' game playing. These included force feedback aircraft joysticks and racing wheel/pedal kits, which allowed home systems to approach the level of realism and immersion available in the arcade.

Many arcades never recovered from their dwindling customers and were forced to close down. The gap these closures left were partly filled by large amusement centres dedicated to providing clean, safe environments and expensive game control systems not available to home users.

These newer arcade titles are usually based on sporting games such as skiing or cycling, as well as rhythm games like Dance Dance Revolution and shooting gallery games such as Time Crisis, which have dominated a large majority of the market.

Today, Dave & Buster's and GameWorks are two large chains in the United States with this type of environment. Aimed at adults and older kids, they feature full service restaurants with full liquor bars and have a wide variety of video game and hands on electronic gaming options. Chuck E. Cheese's – founded in 1977 by whom else but Nolan Bushnell – is a similar type of establishment focused towards younger children.

Chapter 4

The Most Influential Video Games Ever

Donkey Kong (1981) & Super Mario Bros. (1986)

A new console called the ColecoVision, created by toy company Coleco, arrived in August 1982. More advanced than the groundbreaking Atari 5200, the console came with a copy of a game that would firmly put Nintendo on the map: Donkey Kong.

The game was the first to be designed by the man who would go on to become one of video games' greatest ever designers, Shigeru Miyamoto, and is one of the most iconic video games of all time. The game was commissioned

on the back of Nintendo's unsuccessful venture Space Invaders-inspired game Radar Scope. The game was a big hit in Japan, but in the US it had sold only half of the machines that had built for the American market.

As a result, Nintendo decided to create a new game to run on the Radar Scope that could help to sell the remaining machines. The game was originally going to be based on Popeye, but when Nintendo couldn't secure the rights, Miyamoto came up with a new concept inspired by King Kong and Beauty and the Beast.

His idea centred around three charac-

ters: the eponymous giant ape, who acted as the game's main villain; Jumpman, a chubby, moustachioed carpenter who leapt around and saved the day; and Pauline, the object of Jumpman and Donkey Kong's affections. Unlike Pac-Man, Donkey Kong was less a maze-chase game than the game that ushered in the platforming genre that Nintendo would go onto perfect in later years. Players had to help Jumpman rescue the princess by climbing ladders and scaffolding while dodging barrels thrown by the gorilla and other dangers.

The distinctive characters (the titular ape and his nemesis Mario are probably the only gaming characters of their day which could hold their own against Pac-Man) and love triangle were revolutionary, while the game's jumping action and platform-based levels were equally influential, inspiring a new genre of game – the platform game.

By Easter 1983, more than one million ColecoVisions had been sold off thanks to Donkey Kong and the game's legendary status was secured.

LEFT Donkey Kong arcade at the QuakeCon 2005

However, while the iconic gorilla went on to see a plethora of sequels created in his name, the game's other main character did not retreat into the gaming shadows; instead enjoying spin-off success of his own.

The character of Jumpman underwent something of an evolution after Donkey Kong, changing profession and name to become a plumber called Mario for the 1983 arcade platform game Mario Bros.

The name change occurred when Nintendo's US office, who were trying to think of a better name in time for the American release of the game, were interrupted by their landlord Mario Segale, after whom they christened the character. Designed by Miyamoto and Game Boy-creator Gunpei Yokoi, Mario Bros was set in the New York sewer system and also introduced Mario's brother Luigi.

Mario's look was a direct result of the graphical limitations of the hardware at the time. He has a hat, because realistic hair was difficult to portray, a moustache to accentuate his nose, and dungarees to make his arm movements more noticeable.

Eventually he landed his own game and in 1985 Super Mario Bros. was released. The game took the Italian out of his single-screen setting and into a huge, vivid, two-dimensional world, where players had to fight flying turtles and little mushroom men to help Mario rescue a damsel in distress called Peach Toadstool from a dragon called Bowser.

The game also boasted an iconic soundtrack composed by Nintendo's Koji Kondo. The main theme, known as Ground Theme, is one of the most recognisable pieces of game music ever recorded and remained in the Billboard ringtone charts for 125 weeks.

LEFT Donkey Kong Game & Watch

BELOW Mario Bros. Game & Watch

THE MOST INFLUENTIAL VIDEO GAMES EVER

Super Mario Bros.' infectious sense of humour, cartoon-like graphics and fast action, plus hidden "Easter eggs", made the game a huge success in Japanese arcades and soon began to attract some attention in the failing American arcade industry. By the end of the year, Nintendo had created a home version of the game for the Famicom (NES) and packed the game and the console together in Japan.

This move proved so successful that Nintendo created an American version of the game, and to establish a stronger

foothold in the US, Nintendo joined forces with toy company Worlds of Wonder and the game was available by the time Nintendo of America went national at the end of 1986.

The marketing power Nintendo received from teaming with Worlds of Wonder helped greatly to open doors to retailers, doors which remained closed to Sega. As a result, the NES and its included Super Mario Bros game flew off the shelves.

Super Mario Bros.' sequel, Super Mario Bros 2, was designed as a tougher version of the first game and released to support the Famicom Disk System, a new add-on for the Japanese version of the Nintendo Entertainment System. However, it was considered too difficult for Western release, so America and Europe got a tweaked version of the 1987 title Yume Kojo: Doki Doki Panic instead.

The game was hastily refitted with Mario

BELOW Super Mario Bros. Game & Watch

characters in a kind of digital cut-and-shut job. In 1993, the genuine Super Mario Bros. 2 was finally released in the West as Super Mario Bros: the Lost Levels, part of the Super Mario All-Stars collection.

After Super Mario Bros 2 failed to match the brilliance of Miyamoto and Tezuka's original effort, their creators were determined not to make the same mistakes again, and Super Mario Bros 3 represented something of a creative comeback from the lauded duo.

The game revived the sense of wonder that made the original such a wondrous game, and introduced a wave of new features into the Mario world. With the special Super Leaf of Tanooki suit and an exciting array of fun disguises, players could experience Mario flying in the air.

Other key power-ups included Kurribo's Shoe, which allowed the player to hop into a giant shoe

and mercilessly stomp on enemies, plus the fabled Warp Whistle, which could send you to certain points in the game. Super Mario Bros 3 was a seminal release and is regarded as a gaming classic. The game sold more than 17 million copies around the globe and grossed more than $550 million, and in 1990 the franchise received the ultimate seal of approval when the Q Score survey, which measured the popularity of celebrities and brands, concluded that the Italian plumber was now even more famous and popular than Mickey Mouse.

BELOW An classic Nintendo Entertainment (NES) System complete with a Super Mario Bros. sticker

The success of the game represented the end of Nintendo's journey from little-known Japanese toy manufacturer to worldwide video game behemoth. The company had almost single-handedly brought consoles back from the brink and reinvigorated the American games industry, turning it from a $100 million business in 1986 to a $4 billion behemoth in 1991.

However, Nintendo didn't rest on its Super Mario Bros laurels. In 1992 the next instalment, titled Super Mario World was released. Now available on the Super Nintendo Entertainment System (SNES), the game introduced fans to the loveable dinosaur character Yoshi, who quickly became an excellent sidekick to Mario.

In 1997's Super Mario 64, Mario went 3D, becoming the first video game character to have complete movement

BELOW A Super NES and Super Mario World at Festival du Jeu Vidéo

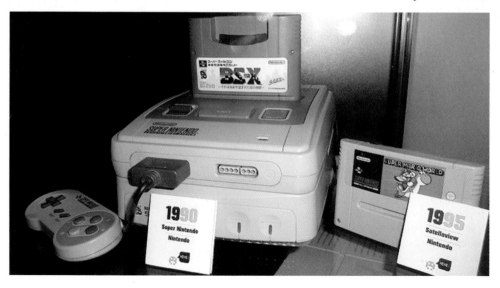

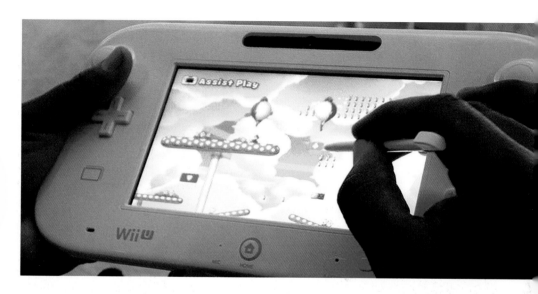

in a 360-degree, three-dimensional home video game environment. Then, in 2002 came the release of Super Mario Sunshine, which marked the first true Mario game on Nintendo GameCube. In the game, Mario is given unprecedented freedom of movement as he tries to clean up Delfino Island.

In 2009, the classic two-dimensional adventure arrived on Wii and for the first time in the history of the Super Mario series, players could either cooperate or compete in simultaneous multiplayer with up to four players.

The Super Mario Bros series is in the Guinness Book of Records as the most successful gaming franchise of all time, boasting global sales of more than 240 million units. More than a quarter of a century since the world was introduced to the famous Italian plumber, his lustre shows no sign of diminishing.

ABOVE Super Mario is still going strong today. Here's Super Mario Bros 2 U being played on the Wii U GamePad

Tetris (1984)

In 1984, a gifted young artificial intelligence researcher at the Soviet Academy of Sciences in Moscow by the name of Alexey Pajitnov received his first desktop computer, the antiquated Elektronika 60. The machine was the Russian clone of the American PDP-11 (programmable Data Processor) and Pajitnov wasted no time in writing programs for it.

But rather than write numerical ones, he instead ended up creating a game (with the help of talented hacker Vadim Gerasimov) that would become one of the most addictive and lauded of all time.

The concept was simple: from the top of the screen a series of differently shaped "blocks" fall slowly towards the bottom. The player can turn each block as it falls – making a line into a column, for example – or move it sideways, but once it hits the lowest point, it stays. If the blocks fill a line without gaps, they disappear. Otherwise they pile up, giving the player less and less time before they hit the "bottom".

Unfortunately for Pajitnov, the game's early success didn't leave him financially better off as the game's rights were owned by the Soviet state. But it was in 1988 that things started to accelerate, when Henk Rogers, a Dutch games publisher who was based in Japan, saw the game at January's Consumer

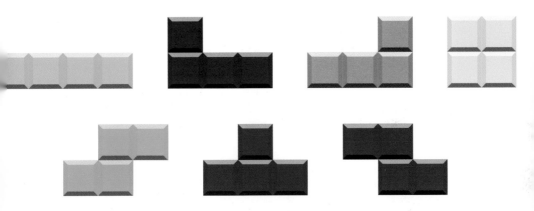

ABOVE Tetrominoes

Electronics Show in Las Vegas. It didn't take Rogers long to realise this deceptively enthralling puzzle game had potential.

"My first impression was that this game was too simple, that there was nothing to it. Then I came back and played it again," said Rogers. "Soon I realised there was something going on – no game had grabbed me at a show just like that."

The Dutchman beat fierce competition to agree a deal that eventually led to an agreement brokered with Nintendo of America. This shrewd move from Nintendo of America's president Minoru Arakawa saw Tetris as the cartridge that was bundled with every Game Boy.

It was the perfect match and the impact of this deal was almost immediate. With the game's simple graphics lending themselves perfectly to the Game Boy's LCD screen, and a style ideal for travel and quick breaks, the game began selling in its millions.

However, while Rogers made a career out of licensing Tetris to other com-

panies around the world, its creator had to wait until 1996 – when the rights reverted to him from the Russian state – to begin making money from his success. By then he had moved to America, where he worked at Microsoft as a games designer.

These days, both men spend their time licensing Tetris to other companies. Between them, they maintain the "Tetris guidelines" – a surprisingly exacting basic standard that any official version of the game must meet.

This includes, among other things, the size of the playing area, the colours of the tetronimos, the configuration of keys and buttons used to move the blocks. Also in the rules is the demand that the game must include a version of the Tetris theme song, Korobeiniki; a song that has become almost as recognisable as the game itself.

Pajitnov, who says he is still a coder at heart, believes that Tetris is a "good program" with simplicity and portability as crucial assets. "Frankly, I think that most of the classic games which were written in the 1980s or early 1990s are dead just

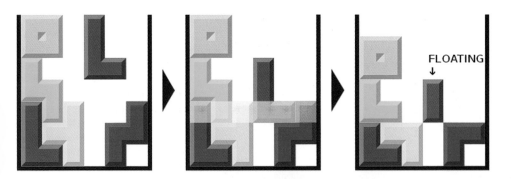

because their authors or owners didn't care about them," he says. "They're still interesting to people, especially now with the new boom of casual games."

Even after so many years – and despite recognising the addictive nature of the game early on – many people, Rogers included, remain surprised that Tetris has displayed such durability.

When you consider that out of all of Tetris' contemporaries, only Nintendo's infamous Italian plumber has shown similar longevity – and even he has changed over the years, the game's durability is astounding. Nearly thirty years since its creation, Tetris has a

ABOVE Behavior after a line clear in Tetris, using the common "naive gravity"

LEFT One of the many Tetris inspired handheld brick games

FAR LEFT Alexey Pajitnov

legitimate claim to being the video game that has truly conquered the world.

In all its forms, the game has sold more than 75 million copies around the globe; it has spawned architecture, art and music; it has earned multiple Guinness World records; and is regularly voted one of the top games of all time.

BELOW Tetris on an ipod

Rogers believes the reason for the game's success lies first with its simple yet addictive play and the fact that despite years of intensive effort no one else has managed to conjure up a better Tetris.

Doom (1993)

Developed by pioneering Texan video game company Id, Doom was a land-mark first-person shooter that shook up the entire video game industry. The game represented a bold move by the youthful studio: its ambition was to create a game that would make its previous success Wolfenstein 3D pail in comparison.

A true team effort, Doom was created by legendary programmers John Carmack and John Romero, game designer Tom Hall and artist Adrian Carmack (no relation), and was a phenomenon unlike any PC game before or after it. In short, video games were never the same after Doom.

Doom was a game about one thing and one thing only: survival. Its simple scenario consisted of players stepping into the head of a marine based on Mars where demons from hell were attacking. The player's job – quite simply – was to kill each and every one of them. To help players do this, an impressive array of weapons ranging from shotguns and rocket launchers to chainsaws was made available.

Doom's action, groundbreaking 3D visuals and artwork alone would have been enough to send shockwaves through the video game business, but Id's game came with one extra selling point that simply rewrote the rules of the industry.

Inspired by the fact that some Wolfenstein 3D fans had hacked into the game and created new versions with new graphics and levels (a practice known as 'modding' – as in modification), Id decided it was time the players had access to its technology.

Such a practice was usually frowned on by other companies, but Id embraced the notion and gave fans unprecedented access to the code that made Doom tick, meaning fans could redesign the game as they wished and share their work. This technique

And that wasn't all. Doom also demonstrated the entertainment power of multiplayer games. One of the game's best options was to let players fight each other rather that go after demons and monsters. They could do this by connecting their computers together

in battles fellow creator John Romero called 'death matches'.

ABOVE Doom gameplay

This concept had been tried before but Doom's arrival coincided with the arrival of the internet, which meant computers could be connected via phone lines rather than direct cables. Using revolutionary viral marketing techniques years, Id kept its insatiable fan base in a state of fervour with a constant drip-feed of information about the cool features that would be in Doom. By launch day the fans were at fever pitch.

The stampede to download the game as soon as it appeared crashed the website's servers several times. Within five months of its launch, Doom's free demo had been downloaded more than a million times and the company was raking in $100,000 a day as fans began buying access to the rest of the game.

The game made Id the hottest video game company in the world and turned its creators into video game superstars. With a personality more suited to being a rock star and the in-depth knowledge and passion that only one of the game's creators could possibly display, Romero was the perfect front man for both the company and the game. It was a role he took relish in playing.

The game had a massive impact on the entire industry, first acting as the catalyst for video gaming's seismic shift from 2D to 3D visuals, setting the standard by which games such as Duke Nukem 3D, Jedi Knight and Descent would be judged.

However, it also changed video games in more subtle but equally revolutionary ways. Id's willingness to break with tradition and embrace 'modding' evolved into a multi-faceted movement responsible for creating hit games, not to mention acting as a training ground for a multitude of game developers.

Plus, their readiness to let other game companies licence its technology was the starting point of a culture shift that led to a widespread exchange of technology between developers in America and Europe.

However, by the end of the decade, the Id team was no more. The fun, dynamic that existed in the studio's early days had changed and the once watertight friendship of Romero and John Carmack had broken down. Shortly after the 1996 release of Doom follow-up Quake, Romero left to form his own studio with Hall.

Despite the breakup of this impressive ensemble, nothing can diminish what they achieved. Twenty years since its release, Doom's impact is still being felt today. First person shooters are the most popular genre in video gaming – and a significant reason for this is Doom.

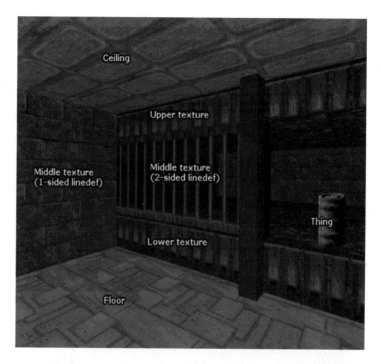

ABOVE Doom map format screen

Call of Duty (2003)

A cultural icon, phenomenally successful and one of the most critically acclaimed franchises in video gaming history, Call of Duty is a first-person and third-person shooter.

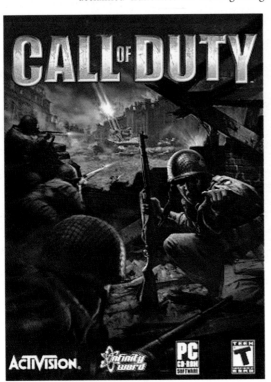

Published and owned by Activision, the studio Infinity Ward has primarily developed the numerous Call of Duty games, but Treyarch has also developed several of the titles, with the release of the studios' games interlaced with each other.

Originally positioned as a direct competitor to EA's Medal of Honor, the first Call of Duty was also based in the military world of the Second World War. However, where Medal of Honor would focus on the heroics of a single US soldier, Call of Duty expanded the focus to capture a startling sense of global conflict, putting you in the shoes of American, British and Russian soldiers.

The multiple viewpoint narrative has become a theme of Call of Duty, and while the original may seem positively conservative when compared to the latest versions of the game, many of Call of Duty's cinematic staples can be traced back to the first game.

Both its campaign and multiplayer feature set a solid basis for a video game series that would become one of the most successful entertainment franchises in the entire world.

An expansion pack for the original game developed by Gray Matter Interactive, United Offensive included new single-player missions, including a new American campaign taking place in the famous Belgian chokepoint of Bastogne. United Offensive's greatest additions, however, were in multiplayer. United Offensive first introduced the idea of ranks into Call of Duty, with players ranking up and claiming new benefits the more they played.

While the original Call of Duty was only available on PC, Activision assigned Spark Interactive to make a spin-off for home consoles PS2, GameCube and Xbox. Finest Hour was the result, a competent but hardly spectacular sideshow to the far superior main attraction of the PC version.

Featuring six intertwined storylines

from soldiers across the globe, the game was faithful to the Call of Duty legacy. It also had 32-man online multiplayer for Xbox, an impressive number for a console generation that was yet to truly embrace online multiplayer.

ABOVE U.S. Air Force Senior Airman Justin Kiel, left, and Airman 1st Class Colin Landry playing Call of Duty video game

The sequels

While at a base level Call of Duty 2 simply followed and improved upon its predecessor, the impact of Infinity Ward's second foray into the Second World War cannot be understated.

The game came as a launch title with Microsoft's new Xbox 360, and while Halo 2 had put the idea of online multiplayer shooters at the forefront of the minds of a mainstream console audience, Call of Duty 2 brought a more austere PC sensibility with its online component.

Players adored the authentic cat-and-mouse matches set in an authentic theatre of war and Call of Duty became the best selling launch title for the new console. The campaign was a huge improvement too, improving enemy AI and ramping up the cinematic impact with evocative ground rushes on D-Day on the shores of Normandy, and tanks rumbling through the barren sands of Africa.

The sequel was also when the series introduced the notion of recharging health. While the system was largely a lift from Halo, Call of Duty arguably popularised the scheme to the extent that it's now the de facto health system in video games.

While Call of Duty 2 was a launch title for Xbox 360, this spin-off was created for the previous generation of hardware, PS2, Gamecube and the original Xbox. Big Red One is notable for being Treyarch's first foray into the Call of Duty series, working with United Offensive developer Gray Matter.

Unlike most Call of Duty games, Big Red One focused on a single Allied squad: the US Army's 1st Infantry Division: the titular Big Red One. Largely a sequel to Call of Duty: Finest Hour, Big Red One could never possibly compete with Call of Duty 2. However, the game was better received than Finest Hour. Treyarch's work certainly didn't go unnoticed, as they would go on to become a key part of the Call of Duty legacy.

The development of Call of Duty 3 was handed to Treyarch and the game was criticised in some quarters for being unvaried and uninspired. However, much praise was heaped on the multiplayer, which introduced vehicles and some excellent game modes.

While Call of Duty's seemingly unstoppable momentum was gathering year on year, it wasn't until the first Modern Warfare that the series was catapulted beyond the confines of gaming circles and into a wider mainstream consciousness.

The shift from the Second World War into modern day conflicts was an inspired move, and Modern Warfare set the bar for which all future online multiplayer shooters would be judged, with its killstreaks and RPG style upgrade system.

Its campaign was praised for its compelling storytelling, throwing the player from one spectacular set-piece to the next in a rollercoaster ride. The difference between this and previous games in the franchise was that

Infinity Ward was now free from the facts of history and able to craft their own story, and its presentation of mod-

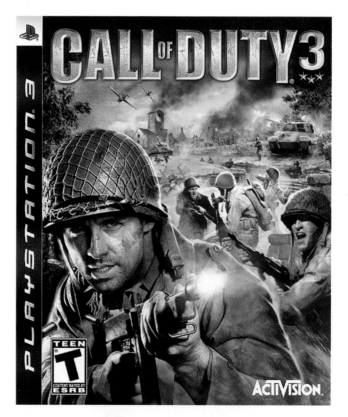

BELOW Call of Duty 3 cover art

ern day heroes was remarkably timely.

As more and more people were converted to the Call of Duty cause, it became clear that video games would never be quite the same again.

With Infinity Ward's focus now concentrated on the Modern Warfare brand, it was down to Treyarch to take the series back to the Second World War; this time focusing on the conflict in the Pacific. However, World at War never escaped the shadow of Modern Warfare, and many felt the return to the Second World War was a step backwards.

By the time Modern Warfare 2 rolled around in 2009, the Call of Duty brand had become a leviathan. Video games were now the most valuable entertainment medium in the world, and Call of Duty was its figurehead.

Buoyed by the huge success of the first Modern Warfare, its sequel arrived on an unprecedented wave of hype. In gameplay terms, Modern Warfare 2 was the expected refinement of the first Modern Warfare. The explosions were bigger, the storyline more out-landish and the scripting tighter, and the multiplayer, which built on the foundations of the first game, cemented Modern Warfare's position as the best multiplayer shooter around. The game was an extraordinary success across the globe, selling more than 20 million copies.

The annual handover to Treyarch came with even more pressure in 2010. As Call of Duty continued to grow, many saw Treyarch's games as pale imitations of Infinity Ward's. However, in 2010 trouble hit Infinity Ward, with studio heads Vince Zampella and Jason West being fired by Activision for breach of contract. It felt like it was the time for Treyarch to step out of the shadows and to many extents, they responded in emphatic fashion.

Rather than returning yet again to the Second World War, Black Ops had a fascinating stab at a psychological storyline based during the Cold War, with flashbacks to Vietnam. It was quite the departure for Call of Duty, but the gameplay was still the spectacular rollercoaster the series has always provided. Black Ops continued Call of Duty's

LEFT Call of Duty Black Ops II artwork

seemingly unstoppable growth, grossing more than $1 billion worldwide. It was also named as the UK's most popular entertainment product of 2010, beating film and music by some margin.

Today, the juggernaut continues to roll on. With the rebuilt Infinity Ward joined by the newly formed Sledgehammer Games, Modern Warfare 3 is set to be the biggest and best entry in the franchise. It will draw a close to the Modern Warfare storyline amidst the death and destruction of The Third World War, while the multiplayer will undergo its most dramatic revamp since Call of Duty 4.

All eyes will be on this to not only repeat the success of its forebears, but build on it. The only true question is: where on Earth will it go next?

Street Fighter II:
The World Warrior (1991)

What Space Invaders was to shooting games, Street Fighter II was to fighting games. Hadoken! Shoryuken! Tatsumaki Senpukyaku!...To this day, every gamer who loved fighting games

BELOW Street Fighter II cover art

can recall the exact button inputs for each of these moves, and it's all because of Street Fighter II, one of the most successful fighting games of all time.

Capcom's Street Fighter I, despite possessing some of the elements that would make its sequel a hit, suffered from poor controls that rendered it almost unplayable. Its 1991 follow-up, however, transformed the one-on-one fighting game that Technos' Karate Champ had pioneered nearly a decade earlier.

Taking inspiration from Hong Kong kung-fu films, Street Fighter II solidified the fighting game formula: two fighters, two lifebars, six buttons, go! It featured colourful characters and cool, complicated moves that made it a game of skill, speed and strategy.

The two-dimension fighting game featured only eight selectable fighters, but the silky-smooth combos (a mechanic mimicked in a plethora of fighting games since) and hidden special moves made it a hit amongst competitive gamers.

The game's gigantic success put Capcom

on the map and propelled the fighting game community into the gaming spotlight. Arcades were dominated by fighting games throughout the 1990s, and rival studios made exciting brawlers of their own (such as SNK's The King of Fighters). In fact, Street Fighter II was so popular that Nintendo designed the Super Nintendo Controller with enough buttons to play the game's home version.

Sadly, Street Fighter II's further sequels were nowhere near as impressive and when the franchise made the move to 3D it didn't bode well for the genre. The previous worldwide success of the series rapidly diminished as younger gamers became more accustomed to the likes of Tekken and Soul Calibur.

ABOVE Cosplayers portraying various characters from Street Fighter at FanimeCon 2010 in San Jose, California

ABOVE Mortal Kombat menu graphics

Mortal Kombat (1992)

When Mortal Kombat was released in 1993, a year after Street Fighter II, arcades were already overflowing with fighting games and some arcade owners were already tiring of them. However, the release of Mortal Kombat changed all that.

In essence, the game wasn't all that different from other beat-'em-ups on the market. Developed by Ed Boon and John Tobias for Midway, Mortal Kombat boasted layer upon layer of two-player action, tactical fighting, special moves and hidden extras, but the aspect that really set it aside from all previous fighting games was one thing: the "Fatalities".

At the end of each fight, the loser would stand, stunned, while a voice boomed "Finish him!"; the winner then had the opportunity to do his finishing move, all of which were particularly gruesome. "We certainly weren't out to cause controversy," said Tobias. "We were out to serve the needs of our players and our number one goal all of the time was to make sure that they enjoyed themselves while playing."

The game was an instant success and easily eclipsed Street Fighter II in overall popularity in America. The home version went on sale on September 13, 1993 ("Mortal Monday") and the sales were stratospheric. The unedited version, which came out on Sega's Genesis, outsold the edited-down Super NES version by nearly three to one. This propelled sales of the Genesis console to new heights.

LEFT Cosplay of Mortal Kombat's Scorpion

THE MOST INFLUENTIAL VIDEO GAMES EVER

However, the game's intense violence inevitably led to moral outrage, which in turn led to hearings in the United States Congress. The hearings turned the Senate into a battleground, where not only video game restrictions were being debated but also Nintendo and Sega – courtesy of Nintendo of America chairman Howard Lincoln and Sega of America vice-president Bill White Jr – were laying down their bitterness towards each other for all to see.

The result of these hearings was that the entertainment software industry was given 12 months to form a working rating system or the federal government would intervene and create its own.

Eventually, the Entertainment Software Rating Board was conceived. This independent organisation rated all video games and the ratings were to be placed on the games' packaging. Mortal Kombat was the first game to receive a mature ESRB rating.

When the time came to develop Mortal Kombat's inevitable sequel, Boon and Tobias made a basic but amusing modification. The developers added a finishing move called "Friendship", where instead of

BELOW Cosplay of Mortal Kombat video game characters, from left to right Kitana, Reptile, and Sonya Blade

decapitating the loser, the winner would present him or her with a bouquet of flowers.

With the ratings in place Nintendo's presidents Howard Lincoln and Minoru Arakawa decided that Nintendo no longer needed to sanitise games the way it had previously. The Super NES version of Mortal Kombat 2 contained as many fatalities and friendships as Sega's version – and, tellingly, it sold more copies than the Genesis version.

Grand Theft Auto III (2001)

One of the most influential not to mention notorious video games of all time, Grand Theft Auto has always been so much more than simply a driving game.

Originally created as an open world game for PC and Sony PlayStation by DMA Design in 1997, the series enjoyed modest success with the first two entries in the franchise, but the breakthrough came with the seminal 3D Grand Theft Auto III for the PlayStation 2.

Released in October 2001, Grand Theft Auto III's 3D city teemed with life and offered a sense of freedom and possibility that no game had come close to achieving before, including the first two Grand Theft Auto games themselves.

The first Grand Theft Auto was created by Mike Dailly and Dave Jones, who had the idea to produce a game where the emphasis was on the player being a bad guy fleeing from the police.

The game was released in October 1997 and its key feature of a city to roam around in went largely ignored. Its overhead viewpoint disappointed many who craved the new high of 3D gameplay. Not only that but the franchise was targeted by tabloids and rightwing pressure groups for its depiction of casual violence.

However, it did catch the imagination of those who recognised that the game

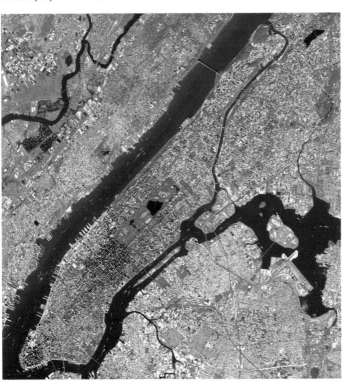

BELOW Manhattan Island arial photo - GTA Liberty City

was a rare example of an action game that took up the challenge presented by Elite and Sim City to give players the chance to create their own storylines through their actions and choices.

But 1999's Driver – modelled on 1970s police shows, primarily Starsky and Hutch had made Grand Theft Auto look outdated already. So, with two impressive but underwhelming entries in the Grand Theft Auto story, its creators DMA Design knew they needed something to knock players off their seats. They needed to deliver a 3D version of their game.

The breakthrough came from a team of DMA employees who had just completed work on Space Station Silicon Valley, a 3D platform game for the Nintendo 64. Their attitude and creative ability saw the GTA franchise make the successful leap into the 3D world and with the addition of a licensed CD soundtrack, Grand Theft Auto III, like Doom before it, reshaped the video game landscape.

And it wasn't just the groundbreaking 3D technology that set Grand Theft

Auto III aside from its contemporaries. The game's open-world gameplay let players follow the story or go off on their own and cause chaos around a thriving metropolis.

It was this chaotic gameplay that helped GTA II become the landmark PlayStation 2 blockbuster, as the chance to fight random passers by, jack cars and be chased by the police allowed gamers to play out all their dark fantasies, and set the model for Saints Row 2 and Yakuza 3

Plus, Grand Theft Auto III was also one of the first games to realise the potential in hiring famous actors to voice some of the characters. Actors such as Robert Loggia, Michael Madsen, Kyle MacLachlan and Joe Pantoliano lent their dulcet tones to the game and there is no doubt that their involvement helped the game's seismic impact.

Having proved they had what it takes to produce a groundbreaking piece of work, Rockstar North – as DMA Design was renamed in 2002 – set about improving on their model in their follow-up, Grand Theft Auto: Vice City.

ABOVE Ricky Gervais features in Grand Theft Auto IV

Auto IV, which had taken a team of approximately 150 people four years to make, that the series' success went stratospheric. Arguably the best written entry in the series, Grand Theft Auto IV not only delivered the promised leap into even greater visual detail but the redesigned Liberty City felt more alive and real than ever before.

Plus, the series' impressive celebrity voices went to the next level with the involvement of Ricky Gervais, who portrayed himself in the game performing a stand-up routine at the game's comedy club.

The game was a staggering success, selling more than 13 million copies and making it one of the biggest hits of the year. However, its scale, bold vision and ambition were what truly caught the attention.

Inspired by iconic 80s American TV show Miami Vice, players were transported into a retro decade of yuppies, drugs and rolled-up sleeves. The game was a massive success, as was the next entry in the series, Grand Theft Auto: San Andreas.

However, it was with Grand Theft

To date, the series as a whole has sold more than 110 million copies worldwide. In 2012, the Grand Theft Auto video game series was selected for inclusion in the British Design 1948–2012: Innovation in the Modern Age exhibition at the Victoria and Albert Museum.

LEFT Grand Theft Auto
IV advertising

On January 31, 2013, Rockstar announced that Grand Theft Auto V would miss its original spring launch window, and would be released on September 17, 2013. Proving that Rockstar's capacity for ambition remains unrivalled, the game will be set in Los Santos and feature three very different criminals seeking to pull off a series of daring heists.

The world will be even vaster than usual, taking in a whole city as well as mountain ranges, deserts and outback towns and characters will have unprecedented freedom – flying helicopters, scuba diving, even playing sports.

Either way, there seems to be more tales left to tell in the Grand Theft Auto story.

Chapter 5

Glossary of Video Game Types

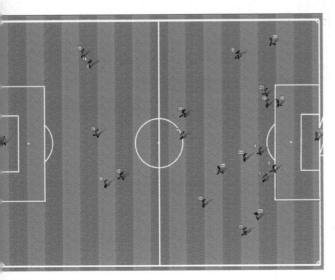

A definitive listing of all of the myriad video game styles would prove too complex. However, here is an overview of some of the most recognised gaming categories, plus some famous examples of each genre.

SPORT

Arguably the broadest category in all of gaming, almost every sporting discipline has been represented in the history of video games. Classics include:

Football Manager (1982)
Acknowledged as the first football management simulation, Football Manager spawned several sequels and

sold more than one million copies. Players were required to choose a team and attempted to be promoted from the fourth to the top division as well as compete for the FA Cup.

John Madden Football (1988)
Named after the former Super Bowl–winning coach of the Oakland Raiders, the first great American Football game was not released until 1988 due to Madden's insistence that the game be as

realistic as possible. The second version of the game was released in 1990, with annual versions since then, and the series is one of the best selling EA Sports series, second only to FIFA.

Tecmo Super Bowl (1991)
Another US sporting great, modern sports titles owe at least some measure of thanks to Tecmo Bowl. Back in the days of the NES, sports games weren't guaranteed to be all that fun, but Tecmo

ABOVE LEFT John Madden Football 1988 gameplay

ABOVE RIGHT John Madden

LEFT Football Manager FA13

Bowl undoubtedly was. Plus, it was also one of the first games to feature voice acting.

FIFA (1993)

When the series began, football video games such as Sensible Soccer and Kick Off dominated the already competitive market. However, EA Sports' annual multi-gaming systems series has been such a resounding success that by the time FIFA 12 was released it broke the record for the fastest selling sports game ever, boasting more than 3.3 million games sold in its first week of release.

RIGHT Mike Tyson's Punch Out!! gameplay

BELOW Fifa International Soccer gameplay

Mike Tyson's Punch Out!! (1987)

Mike Tyson's Punch Out!! was a home adaptation of Nintendo's arcade boxing classic, released in 1983. The home version featured twice as many opponents as the arcade game, including the recently crowned heavyweight champion of the world, Mike Tyson.

Fighting as Little Mac, the diminutive but brave boxer, players had to battle their way through numerous amusingly named fighters, including Soda Popinski and Mr. Sandman, to reach the ultimate goal: to fight Iron Mike Tyson for the World Video Boxing Association Title. It went on to become a million-selling game for Nintendo.

Tony Hawk's Pro Skater series (1999) Originally released for the PlayStation and later ported to the Nintendo 64, Dreamcast, and N-Gage, Activision's Pro Skater was a groundbreaking series that ruled every console it appeared on.

Its addictive game playing challenged players to perfect precise tricks in prescribed places or reach seemingly inaccessible areas, the series highpoint was arguably 2002's Pro Skater 4. The series lost its edge slightly after that, but 2012's nostalgic HD version of the game saw the franchise stage a successful comeback.

ABOVE Tony Hawk and Tony Hawk's Pro Skater series cartridges for Nintendo 64

FIGHTING

This self-explanatory video game genre requires players to control an on-screen character and engage in close combat with an opponent. Players must master techniques such as blocking, counter-attacking, and chaining together sequences of attacks known as "combos".

Kung-Fu Master (1984) and
Karate Champ (1984)

The fighting genre really took off in 1984 with the arrival of these two ground-breaking games. Both Kung-Fu Master and Karate Champ were inspired by the iconic Bruce Lee karate films of the 1970s, such as The Big Boss and Game of Death.

Data East's Karate Champ pitted players against a computer or second person in a one on one bout of combat. Alternatively, Kung-Fu Master from Irem challenged players to battle through hordes of attacks on a personal journey to reach a final defining conflict.

Released within weeks of each other, these two games provided the blueprint for almost every subsequent fighting, including Final Fight, Double Dragon and Street Fighter.

Street Fighter II:
The World Warrior (1991)

Originally released in arcades before hitting homes worldwide in 1992, Street Fighter II is widely credited for kick-starting the fighting genre.

By 1994, the game that gave us Ken, Blanka, Balrog and Zangief, had been played by more than 25 million Americans in arcades and homes by 1994. It remains Capcom's best-selling consumer game of all time.

Mortal Kombat (1992)

This game was as hyper violent as it was ground-breaking, and the controversy it created meant its legacy is still felt today.

SHOOT 'EM UPS

The games that helped create the genre – Spacewar! and Space Invaders – need no introduction. However, the genre kicked on and developed with the likes of Galaxian and its sequel Galaga, and 1981 classic, Defender. Plus, Atari released a trip of landmark games: Missile Command, Tempest and I, Robot. Other notable examples of the genre and how it has continued to develop include:

After Burner (1987)

This classic game from Sega involving jet fighter air battles was a gripping ride for fans of the genre.

Max Payne (2001)

This gritty third-person shooter released in 2001 stood out for its excellent 'bullet time' effect, which players to slow time during the intense gun fights. The success of the game saw an equally impressive sequel released two years later, Max Payne 2: The Fall of Max Payne

DRIVING

One of the most popular and enduring of all gaming genres, early driving games were naturally restricted by technology. The seminal arcade coin-op games Nürburgring 1 and Night Driver introduced the concept of driving from the driver's perspective, while Turbo was the first game to use the behind-the-car view.

OutRun (1986)

A classic of its time, Sega's rear-perspec-

tive game is one of the most identifiable driving games of all time. This pioneering game also offered the choice of music to listen to while driving.

Super Mario Kart (1992)

This superb go-karting racing game for up to four players, starring the Mario franchise's best-known characters, spawned the kart-racing genre. The game has aged superbly and is arguably gaming finest spin-off.

Gran Turismo (1997)

Giving you the chance to build a virtual garage with every kind of stylish car possible, PlayStation's racing simula-

tion game debuted in 1997 and boasted pristine graphics and detail so impressive driving fans were immediately hooked.

Grand Theft Auto (1997)

This superb game garnered critical acclaim for its rich and detailed setting Liberty City and arguably popularised the open-world template.

X-Motor Racing (2012)

Featuring high precision physics simulation, online multiplayer and open architecture, this excellent racing simulator game boasts such levels of accuracy that it is used as professional software for driver training. The game is also used for research and development purposes in education, real motor sport and the automotive industry by the likes of Massachusetts Institute of Technology and McGill University.

ABOVE Super Mario Kart gameplay

LEFT X-Motor Racing cover art

SINGLE-PLAYER ROLE-PLAYING GAMES

This genre of video games is a loosely defined style of computer and console game with origins in role-playing games like Dungeons & Dragons, on much of the genre's terminology, settings, and game mechanics is based.

This translation changes the experience of the game, providing a visual representation of the world but emphasising statistical character development over collaborative, interactive storytelling.

Rogue (1980)

Dungeons & Dragons and Pedit5 kick-started the genre but the most enduring of the early games was Rogue. The game's influence and cult following spawned a massive amount of imitators, including Moria, Freedom Force, and NetHack.

Ultima: The First Age of Darkness (1981)

This 1981 release on the Apple II was the first entry in the genre-defining series, but it wasn't until the brilliant Ultima IV: Quest of the Avatar that the bar was truly raised for all role-playing games. The series went on to boast many sequels and spin-offs.

BELOW Rogue Screen Shot

`el:4      Hits:29(29)    Str:16(16)      Gold:718      Armor:5    Exp:4/76`

Baldur's Gate (1998)

This classic release from BioWare represented role-playing game writing at its peak and was largely credited for revitalising the genre.

Mass Effect 2 (2010)

The second entry in the ambitious space opera saga, this stunning sci-fi adventure was an action-packed, role-playing game epic.

JAPANESE ROLE-PLAYING GAMES

This massively influential category boasts some of the most seminal games in video gaming history.

For example:

Legend of Zelda (1986)

The iconic Zelda series skilfully combined a captivating action game with the essence of the role-playing game. Nintendo's first game came out in 1986 and the way it immediately offered gaming without restrictions captivated the gaming public. For many, the best of the series is 1991's memorable A Link to the Past.

ABOVE Final Fantasy XIII Launch

Final Fantasy (1987)

The first game in the series was conceived by its creator Hironobu Sakaguchi as his last-ditch effort in the game industry. However, Final Fantasy was a massive success and spawned many sequels, reaching a high point with Final Fantasy VII. The enthralling stories focus on a group of memorable heroes battling a great evil, while exploring the characters' internal struggles and relationships.

Pokémon (1996)

Created by Satoshi Tajiri, this "collecting, training and battling" classic is the most popular Japanese role-playing game of all time by some distance. An unstoppable video game phenomenon that spread across the globe following its Japanese debut in 1996, Pokémon and its custard-coloured star Pikachu started as a video game but by the time it reached America it had become a multimedia brand.

ADVENTURE

The term 'adventure game' originates from Will Crowther's 1976 computer game Adventure, which, after enjoying a successful remix the following year by Don Woods, pioneered a style of gameplay that was widely imitated and became a genre in its own right. Essential elements of the genre include storytelling, exploration, and puzzle solving.

In the 1980s, Infocom dominated the adventure genre, creating several classics for the Apple II, including Deadline (1982), Planetfall (1983) and Plundered Hearts (1987).

Infocom's biggest rival was Sierra, who delivered the era's other excellent adventure games. These included Time Zone (1982), the King's Quest series (which began in 1984), which introduced animation into adventure games, and the game aimed at all ages, Torin's Passage (1995).

George Lucas' company Lucasfilm (which would become LucasArts) dominated for a 10-year period from the mid 1980s onwards, with perfect exponents of the genre such as Indiana Jones & The Last Crusade (1982), Indiana Jones & The Fate of Atlantis (1992) and Full Throttle (1995).

By 2000, adventure games' popularity had faded. However, although traditional adventure games are rare in today's American market, action-adventure games that combine elements of adventure games with action games are quite common. In Japan, though, adventure games continue to be popular in the form of visual novels, which make up nearly 70 per cent of PC games released in Japan.

LEFT Zelda the Wind Waker

RIGHT Lara Croft
Tomb Raider

ACTION/ARCADE ADVENTURES

Possibly the broadest genre of all, arcade adventure encompasses the story and puzzle solving elements of adventure games with arcade action.

Ghostbusters (1984)
Created on the back of the iconic Bill Murray film, this game proved equally popular with eighties gamers.

Tomb Raider II (1997)
Arguably the best game in the seminal series. The original game, which made a star of its iconic heroine Lara Croft, made its debut on the Sega Saturn, PlayStation, and PC and was one of the major titles responsible for the PlayStation's phenomenal success in the mid-1990s. The second instalment was an astounding commercial success and is considered one of the best selling games of all time

Unchartered:
Drake's Fortune (2007)
This addictive action game owes a massive debt to the Indiana Jones film series and boasted an even more spectacular sequel.

PLATFORM

Platform games originated in the early 1980s and were followed by 3D successors, which became extremely popular in the mid-1990s. The term describes games where jumping on platforms is an integral part of the gameplay and the first game that could truly be described as a platform game was 1980's Space Panic.

However, it was the following year when video gaming would be introduced to the first great example of the genre.

Donkey Kong (1981)

Nintendo's flagship platform classic would go on to outlast even Pac-Man in the decades to come, spawning many sequels.

Super Mario Bros. (1983)

Many developers learned a different lesson from Pac-Man. Rather than borrow its gameplay or structure developers took note of Namco's success in building a game around a strong central mascot. The most famous example of this, next to Pac-Man, is Super Mario Bros. which used its adorable titular character and fantastic platform jumping gameplay to entrance a generation of gamers.

Chuckie Egg (1983)

This was gaming at its most simple yet effective. Chuckie Egg popularised the platform game and sparked different forms on other consoles, including the Commodore 64 and Atari. The game, which is estimated to have sold more than one million copies, required diminutive hero Hen-House Harry to collect 12 eggs positioned in each level before the countdown timer expires.

Sonic The Hedgehog (1991)

As game developers started to move towards consoles and away from the arcade, the power of a well-constructed mascot came into play. Perhaps the best example in this regard is Sonic The Hedgehog, an addictive game where platforming met pinball.

BELOW Sonic The Hedgehog cover art

The iconic hedgehog helped Sega win an early victory in the console wars and proved to be a worthy rival to Nintendo's Mario. However, it was the spectacular loops and corkscrews of its follow-up that proved that Sonic's creators had the same vision. Sonic 2 was one of the best two-player games of the 16-bit era. Another excellent sequel was 1998's Sonic Adventure – which introduced a 3D Sonic to the world.

BELOW Prince of Persia (The Two Thrones 2005)

Prince of Persia (1989)

This superbly designed platform game, represented a massive leap forward in terms of video game animation. The critically acclaimed game was originally released on the Apple II, but it wasn't until it was released in Europe and Japan that Prince of Persia became a commercial success.

After that, the game was ported to various home computers and consoles, eventually selling more than two million copies worldwide and spawning a Hollywood movie adaptation.

PUZZLES

Within this self-explanatory genre there is a large variety of different types of games. Some feed to the player a random assortment of blocks or pieces that they must organise in the correct manner, such as Tetris, while others present a preset game board or pieces and challenge the player to solve the puzzle by achieving a goal.

Sokoban (1982)

This incredibly tough block-pushing

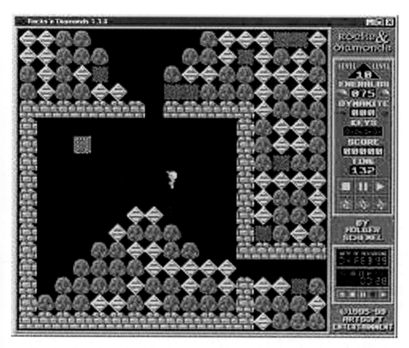

LEFT Boulder Dash gameplay

puzzle game from the early eighties is so challenging that the game was a focus of artificial intelligence researchers.

Boulder Dash (1984)

Based on the 1982 arcade game The Pit, Boulder Dash was originally developed for Atari computers but was later released to other consoles, including Spectrum, Apple II and Commodore 64. The first in a series of sequels, this excellent arcade puzzle game required players to ensure that the hero, Rockford, collects all the diamonds and avoids contact with monsters and falling rocks.

Tetris (1984)

The undisputed king of this genre is Tetris, created by Russian computer engineer Alex Pajitnov. Still as compelling today as it was nearly 30 years ago, the game has many imitators, but has never been bettered. The best of the rest include: Klax, Bejeweled and Puzzle Bobble.

Minesweeper (1990)

Thanks to its inclusion in the Windows operating system, this mine-spotting logic puzzle is one of the world's most played games.

Lemmings (1991)

With its simple premise of saving a plethora of cute yet oblivious lemmings from a multitude of possible deaths, this was a massively popular Amiga game.

MAZE

One of the earliest styles of video games, Maze was a term coined by journalists during the 1980s to describe any game in which the entire playing field was a maze. Quick player action is required to escape monsters, outrace an opponent, or navigate the maze within a time limit.

Pac-Man (1980)

This Namco classic remains the genre's finest moment. When the game first burst onto the arcade scene in 1980, no one could have been prepared for just how successful it would be. Not only did it establish the addictive maze-chase genre of

BELOW Lemmings gameplay

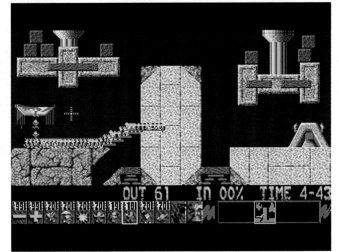

games, it introduced video games to one of its most famous and long-lasting mascots. Pac-Man's influence would be felt in arcade gaming and beyond for decades to come.

Ms. Pac-Man (1981)

The first and most obvious progeny of Pac-Man was Ms. Pac-Man, released in America the year after Pac-Man. The most successful American-produced arcade game of all time, it was essentially the same game as its predecessor, except with faster gameplay, a bigger selection of mazes, intermissions and food-shaped bonus items which bounced around the maze.

Lock 'N' Chase (1981)

This infectious maze chase game from Data East also came hot on the heels of Pac-Man. Players controlled a thief who had to evade capture from roving policemen as they picked up coins in a maze. It was slightly different to Pac Man in that players were able to open and lock off parts of the maze, thus trapping their pursuers.

Dig Dug (1982)

Dig Dug was another interesting

spin on the maze chase genre where players cut their own maze into the environment and weren't boxed in by immovable walls. They were also armed with a pump which could explode any monsters which attack them.

ABOVE Dig Dug gameplay

FIRST-PERSON SHOOTER

Extremely popular and significant in today's gaming world, this is a video game genre that focuses on weapon-based combat with the player experiencing the action through the eyes of the protagonist. Since the genre's inception, advanced 3D or pseudo 3D graphics have challenged hardware development, and multiplayer gaming has been integral.

Wolfenstein 3D (1992)

The genre's origins stretch back to 1974's Maze War, but the world had to wait until Id Software's 1992 classic Wolfenstein 3D before the first-person shooter became a permanent fixture.

RIGHT Halo: Combat Evolved gameplay

Focusing on the simple premise of killing as many Nazis as possible, this game is the basic archetype upon which all subsequent titles were based.

Doom (1993)
Id's Wolfenstein follow-up is quite simply one of the most significant video games ever made. A masterpiece.

GoldenEye 007 (1997)
Based on Pierce Brosnan's debut James Bond film released in 1995, GoldenEye 007 was the first landmark console first-person shooter. Highly acclaimed for its atmospheric single-player levels and well-designed multiplayer maps, the game also boasted an impressive split-screen multiplayer mode, in which two, three or four players could compete in different types of deathmatch games.

For a while in the mid 2000s, it was the best-selling Nintendo 64 game in the US.

Halo: Combat Evolved (2001)
This iconic and thrilling sci-fi block-buster, developed by Bungie and released by Microsoft, was the launch title for the Xbox gaming system.

ABOVE Doom gameplay

Set in the 26th century, the player assumes the role of the Master Chief, a cybernetically enhanced supersoldier, who battles various aliens as they attempt to uncover the secrets of the eponymous Halo, a ring-shaped artificial world.

One of the most important games of the modern gaming era, this game was the starting point for the groundbreaking Halo series, which heightened the console's commercial and critical appeal as a platform for first-person shooter titles.

Halo 2 and Halo 3 proved equally vital inclusions in the franchise and in November 2011 – the 10th anniversary of the original title's launch – an enhanced high definition remake of Halo: Combat Evolved was released.

STEALTH

The idea that gamers could become interested in games that traded on player vulnerability was something that the PlayStation helped to establish as a new entry in the 1990s game-playing vocabulary: the stealth game.

Metal Gear Solid (1998)
This classic from Konami represented the moment when stealth games captured the game playing world's attention. Although Japan-based Tenchu: Stealth Assassins was first to be released, it was Hideo Kojima's test of skill and ingenuity that became the focal point for the genre's birth.

Starring Solid Snake, the definitive video-game tough guy, Metal Gear Solid's avoid-being-seen gameplay inspired such stealth titles as Assassin's

Creed and Splinter Cell, and spawned a number of successful sequels and spin-offs

Assassin's Creed II (2009)
The original Assassin's Creed was regarded as an interesting and beautiful game, but one that failed to grip the player. This superb sequel was expertly reshaped to carry over few of its prede-

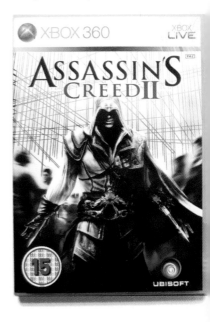

cessor's faults, boasting missions more elaborate and far more enjoyable than original game's. No one would accuse this game of not holding the player's attention.

Batman: Arkham Asylum (2009)
Developed by London-based Rocksteady Studios, few licensed titles have captured so authentically and completely the ethos of its inspiration as Arkham Asylum. The level of attention and invention made this excellent game supremely popular with both fans of the film and the genre.

MUSIC

This category didn't really find its feet until the late 1990s and early 2000s, when a glut of Japanese games dominated the market. These included:

Dance Dance Revolution (1998)
This pioneering series introduced the rhythm and dance genre to video games. Players had to stand on a "dance platform" or stage and hit coloured arrows laid out in a cross with their feet to musical and visual cues and

then be judged as to how well they time their dance to the patterns presented to them.

Guitar Freaks (1999)
Konami's game introduced the guitar controller to the world and is considered one of the most influential video games

ABOVE Dance Dance Revolution North American arcade machine

of all time, having laid the foundations for popular guitar-based rhythm games.

Guitar Hero (2006)

Eventually the US caught up with Japan and Guitar Hero, which combined the music game with those that love to dream of being a rock star by the powers of air guitaring, became a huge success.

BELOW Guitar Hero World Tour Guitar Controller PS3

Rock Band (2007)

This excellent 2007 game, combined singing, guitar-playing and drumming to impressive effect

SURVIVAL HORROR

Inspired by horror fiction, this sub-genre of action-adventure video games sees players challenged to navigate dark maze-like environments, solve puzzles and react to unexpected attacks from enemies.

Although combat is sometimes part of the gameplay, players are made to feel less powerful than in typical action games, due to limited ammunition, health, speed, or other limitations.

Alone in the Dark (1992)

Infogrames' classic PC horror game was one of the first entries in the genre and set the horror video game standard. Forerunner of Alone in the Dark: The

New Nightmare, this 1992 release featured two selectable characters, Edward Carnby and Emily Hartwood, who players had to guide through a creepy 3D mansion with fixed perspectives, much like the game's spiritual descendent Resident Evil.

Resident Evil (1996)

However, it was after 1996's seminal PlayStation and GameCube release of Resident Evil that gamers truly fell in love with video game nasties. Based in Racoon City, where strange disappearances and bizarre murders have seen Special Forces teams sent to investigate, players can choose between two characters, Jill Valentine or Chris Redfield, each with different starting weapons. Trapped in a zombie-filled mansion, players are faced with a fight to get out alive.

ABOVE Resident Evil

By restricting view, movement and ammunition, players were left feeling completely vulnerable against the unholy beasts that were set against them. The benchmark of horror survival, Resident Evil is also the title that pushed the genre into centre stage.

The game has yielded numerous sequels and offshoots but the most significant was Resident Evil 4, which realigned the horror genre by using faster-moving zombies and horrors than the previously shuffling and ominous figures.

Silent Hill (1999)

The first instalment in what would become one of the best-known destinations in the history of horror video games, Silent Hill is an undeniable classic in the survival horror genre.

The game borrowed a host of horror movie techniques, including ominous sound effects and shuffling movements, to highlight the other-worldliness of the game's horrific creatures, and owed much of its signature atmospherics to the constraints of the console it was released on.

RIGHT Silent Hill gameplay

BELOW Resident Evil 2 for Playstation

Other types of games include:
- Simulations
- Pinball
- Strategy and Management
- God games
- Massively Multiplayer Online Role-Playing games
- Virtual Pets
- Social Networking

Chapter 6

The Most Significant Figures in Gaming History

RIGHT Nolan Bushnell, 2009

Nolan Bushnell

In the world of video games Nolan Bushnell is nothing short of an iconic figure, a man whose pioneering efforts conjured the games industry as we know it out of thin air.

Born in Utah in 1943, Bushnell was not responsible for the first video game, nor was he the first to design and sell a home video game console. However, with Computer Space he introduced video games to the arcades, and the company he founded, Atari, was the first to turn games into big business.

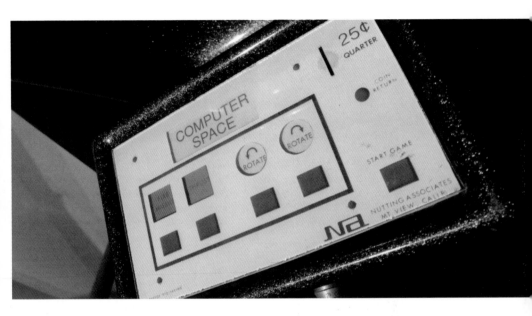

ABOVE Control panel from Arcade game Computer Space

He achieved such a seismic feat, first with the release of Pong in 1972, and then with the introduction of the first console to achieve any measure of success: the Atari 2600,

In 1971, Bushnell and his friend Ted Dabney designed Computer Space, inspired by Spacewar!, and persuaded Nutting Associates to manufacture it. It wasn't a success - 1,500 were sold - as the public found it somewhat baffling. However, Bushnell felt that Nutting Associates had not marketed the game well, and decided that his next game would be licensed to a bigger manufacturer.

Undaunted, Bushnell and Dabney formed Atari in 1972, and hired programmer, Alan Alcorn. The three had developed paper designs for a home console when Bushnell had a sneak preview of the first home console, the Magnavox Odyssey, created by another games industry pioneer, Ralph Baer.

It featured a basic tennis game, which reminded Bushnell of an even earlier effort than Spacewar!: "The very first game was an oscilloscope tennis game by a guy called Willie Higinbotham," explained Bushnell. "We played one of those on the university machine, and seeing the Magnavox kind of reminded me of it. So I said: 'This is not a very fun game - let's make it better.'"

Thus, Pong was born. Alcorn came up with the slightest yet most ingenious of innovations for the game, in that where you hit the ball on the paddle determined the angle at which it comes off. This little tweak turned Pong from a non-game into a game. But Baer wasn't happy and threatened to sue. Bushnell simply licensed the tennis game from him, establishing a practice that remains pivotal in the games industry.

Bushnell sold Atari to Warner Communications in 1976 and the Atari 2600 arrived the following year. However, after fierce disagreements with Warner over its future direction, notably on the lifespan of the 2600 and their closed software strategy, he left both the company, and industry, he founded in November 1978.

Even today, Bushnell feels extremely strongly about the decision he took: "I really saw that they were going to totally screw it up. The only thing that I was wrong about is that it took them two years longer than I thought it would."

By 1982, Atari was boasting $2 billion in annual sales and was the fastest-growing company in the history of American business. However, just two years later the company had crashed and was split into three pieces to be sold off. Bushnell's fears had proved to be prescient.

Bushnell then founded the Chuck E Cheese restaurant chain, which proved to be a roaring success for many years, but money problems soon hit the company. Bushnell had taken a back seat role in the company but tried to step back in to solve the crisis, blaming the money problems on over-expansion, too much tweaking of the formula and saturation in local markets by the management team.

When his proposed changes were rejected by the board of directors, he resigned in February 1984. The company then entered bankruptcy in October 1984. ShowBiz Pizza, a competing pizza/arcade family restaurant, then purchased Chuck E. Cheese's Pizza Time Theatre and assumed its debt.

The newly formed company, ShowBiz Pizza Time, operated restaurants under both brands before unifying all locations under the Chuck E. Cheese's brand. Today more than 500 locations of this restaurant are in business.

Today Bushnell is once more involved with video games, owning a restaurant-gaming business, uWink, which allows people to play games while eating in restaurants, and NeoEdge, which finances the creation of casual games using various methods of advertising.

He has also been inducted into the Video Game Hall of Fame and the Consumer Electronics Association Hall of Fame, received the BAFTA Fellowship and has been named as one of Newsweek's "50 Men Who Changed America".

Alan Turing

The word 'genius' is one that is bandied about with far too much abandon. But if ever the term was truly appropriate, then Alan Turing would be a worthy recipient.

Though best known for the story of his wartime heroism at Bletchley Park and for the appalling circumstances of his death, Turing is also regarded by computer scientists as the father of computer science and artificial intelligence.

LEFT Alan Turing

Born in 1912, Turing studied mathematics at Cambridge University, and it was there in 1936 that he formulated his ideas of the Turing Machine, the "automatic machine" he discussed in a paper and formally extrapolated over the years. At that point, there was not the electronic technology available for him to realise his dream of a computing machine, but the philosophical principles of the Turing Machine power every computer and smartphone today.

The concept would help lay the foundation for future computer science, arguing that a simple machine, given enough tape (or, perhaps more appropriately in the modern sense, storage) could be used to solve complex equations. Turing believed that all that was needed was a writing method, a way of manipulating what is written and a really long ream to write on. In order to increase the complexity, only the storage, not the machine, needs upgrading.

By 1938, he had been headhunted to work at Bletchley Park, which was being established as the wartime codebreaking centre. Here he played a vital role in deciphering the messages encrypted by the German Enigma machine, which provided vital intelligence for the Allies. He took the lead in a team that designed a machine known as a "bombe" that successfully decoded German messages.

After the war, Turing turned his thoughts to the development of a machine that would logically process information. He worked first for the National Physical Laboratory, where, in 1946, he started to design his own calculating machine. He had developed his own ideas on the theory of universal computation, in a complicated paper entitled On Computable Numbers, published in 1936.

Turing submitted the Proposed Electronic Calculator, a document describing what the NPL management were soon calling Ace – the Automatic Computing. Throughout 1946 and 1947, the NPL management made unsuccessful efforts to set up an electronics group to build Turing's paper design for Ace and a disillusioned Turing left to go to Cambridge University for a sabbatical year. However, James Wilkinson took over the project in Turing's absence and in it went into service in late 1951, and saw considerable operational service over the next several years.

The Pilot Ace "automatic computing engine" was the world's first general purpose computer – and for a while was the fastest computer in the world. Today, the Pilot Ace resides at London's Science Museum, where it is heralded as a 20th century icon.

We now take the ability to carry out a range of tasks on our computers for granted, but it all started with the principles developed by Turing in the 1930s and his design for the Ace. It was in many ways groundbreaking, faster than other contemporary British computers by about a factor of five, while employing about one-third of the electronic equipment.

Sadly, Turing died in 1954 at the age of just forty-two. In 1966, the Association for Computing Machinery established the prestigious Turing Award for contributions to computing, while in 1999, Time Magazine named Turing as one of the "100 Most Important People of the 20th Century".

Shigeru Miyamoto

Born in 1952 and hired by Nintendo in 1977, Japanese game designer Shigeru Miyamoto is responsible for some of

LEFT Shigeru Miyamoto

the most innovative, ground breaking and successful work in the history of video gaming.

Not only did Miyamoto bring us Donkey Kong, which would be enough of an accomplishment by itself, but he is also the visionary responsible for the highest-selling video game franchise in history in Super Mario Bros. and The Legend of Zelda, the game that took the niche genre of role-playing games and made them popular.

When Miyamoto was hired by Nintendo it was originally for his artistic capabilities, at a time when arcade titles were still very much the exclusive domain of programmers. However, despite his lack of technical skills, Miyamoto was eventually given the job of designing and overseeing his own game.

Launched in 1981, Miyamoto's creation, Donkey Kong, was a milestone in video games. Not only was it one of the most addictive games of its time but it also was one of the first to feature characters, in this case a plumber called Mario. Interestingly, Mario only gained his striking characteristics due to the lim-

ited graphical capabilities of the time.

And then the arrival of the home Nintendo system in 1985 changed the principles for videogame design forever. The first game on the new machine was the Miyamoto-designed Super Mario Bros,, which introduced the world to countless innovations that today are an essential part of almost every videogame designer's palette. The game has since sold more than 50 million copies and transformed the perception of the video game from that of a passing fad to a powerful entertainment industry.

Since then Miyamoto has worked on more than 60 different Nintendo titles, including another genre-defining game in The Legend of Zelda. His creative abilities turned Nintendo into not only one of the world's most formidable companies but one that brought consoles back from the dead.

In 1998, Miyamoto was honoured as the first person inducted into the Academy of Interactive Arts and Sciences' Hall of Fame, and then in 2006, he was made a Chevalier of the French Ordre des Arts et des Lettres.

Will Wright

Born in Atlanta in 1960, Will Wright is one of video gaming's most influential designers, whose work would define an alternative version of the video gaming. Twenty years ago, a video game where dying and surviving were irrelevant and that you could neither win nor lose was inconceivable – unless you were Will Wright. Inspired by his love of robots and fascination with artificial intelligence and simulation, 24-year-old Wright came up with the idea of creating a game based on designing and building cities, and more importantly, a game for people who simply wanted to play for fun.

It took Wright five years to finally realise his dream but by 1989 his world-building tool Sim City was ready for release. After a slow start, a glowing review in Time magazine prompted a massive surge in sales for Wright's groundbreaking game.

As well as appealing to many video game fans, Sim City also connected with an audience who would normally be disinterested in popular video games such as

LEFT Will Wright at Game Developers Conference 2010

shoot 'em ups and fighting games.

The game spawned a myriad sequels and expansions, and Wright went on to win many awards for his work. His last work, Spore, was released in September 2008 and featured gameplay based upon the model of evolution and scientific advancement.

Wright's success in taking his game into the mainstream of game design also encouraged other designers to start investigating the possibilities. One person inspired was Sid Meier, the co-founder of Microprose, and the man who would go on to create Civilization, the epic fantasy game.

In achieving his goal, Wright created a new genre in gaming and within it, one of the best-loved game franchises in history. It established him as a visionary within the world of video game design and one of the few video game creators to bring gaming to masses. He is undoubtedly one of the most important people in video gaming history and his contributions are still felt today.

Steve Jobs and Steve Wozniak

Two of the most pioneering figures in computer and video gaming history, this tale of the two Steves began at Homestead High School in Cupertino, California. After growing up, appropriately, close to the heart of Silicon Valley, Steve switched to his new school and it was here that Steve Jobs met Steve Wozniak, who was nearly five years older.

Wozniak was a technical wizard who was in and out of college and liked to make machines to show off to other tinkerers. The two hit it off immediately and built and sold "blue boxes" - devices that enabled users to hijack phone lines and make free - and illegal - calls.

After finishing high school in 1972, Jobs moved north to study at Reed, an expensive liberal arts college in Portland, Oregon. He dropped out after one term, but continued to go to some classes, including a course on calligraphy. He worked sporadically as an electronics technician at video game maker Atari, before travelling to India on a quest for enlightenment.

On his return to America, Jobs resumed his job at Atari and was given the task of creating a more compact circuit board for the game Breakout. He had no interest in the intricacies of circuit board design and persuaded his friend Wozniak, to do the job for him, offering to split any bonus fifty-fifty.

Jobs was given $5,000 by a delighted Atari, but Wozniak only got $375 under the impression the payout was $600. Many years later after their business relationship had run its course, Wozniak found out about his friend's deception.

At this point, Jobs with his limited education looked like he was heading nowhere, but he did possess one significant talent: the ability to talk people into things. And he honed this talent to spectacular effect when he persuaded his childhood friend Wozniak, who had by now created a computer circuit board he was showing off to a group of Silicon Valley computer hobbyists, to leave his engineering job so they could design computers themselves.

LEFT Steve Wozniak

In April 1976, the two launched Apple Computer out of Jobs' parents' garage, reproducing Wozniak's circuit board as their first product. They soon became a formidable partnership. On one side you had Jobs with his fierce ambition and, before long, high design standards, impressive ability to make deals and, soon, great marketing skills. On the other, you had Wozniak, the master computer hardware designer.

The first Apple computer was a hobbyist machine in a crude wooden box. It was assembled by hand at Jobs's parents' house and sold for $666.66 because Wozniak liked repeating digits. It made Jobs realise that, in order to compete, Apple had to be set up as a proper company, with financial backing and an experienced chief executive. That happened with an investment from a former Intel employee, Mike Markkula, and the appointment of Apple's first chief executive, Mike Scott.

The following year came Wozniak's follow-up effort, the Apple II, which he designed almost single-handedly. It wasn't all plain sailing, though. During the designing stages, Jobs argued that the Apple II should have two expansion slots, while Wozniak wanted eight of them. After a heated argument, during which Wozniak had threatened for Jobs to 'go get himself another computer', they decided to go with eight slots.

The Apple II also boasted built-in colour graphics and the ability to plug into a TV set. These were significant advantages over rivals that appeared the same year. But Jobs' input wasn't exactly insignificant. Thanks to him, the Apple II also had a strikingly original case, a helpful manual and consumer-friendly advertising.

It was a great success, dominating the US market until the IBM PC was launched in August 1981. Upgraded versions continued to sell for many years.

Its success also enabled Apple Computer to go public in December 1980, with its share price more than doubling on the opening day, valuing the young company at $1.8bn.

Plus, as one of the first personal computers, it had a massive effect on the video game market. For many, it was their first experience with any computer; so the idea there was a box that could function as an automated 'gamemaster' was exciting.

The Apple II was responsible for introducing the world to the likes of Castle Wolfenstein., Wizardry: Proving Grounds of the Mad Overlord, fantasy role-playing classic Ultima and Lode Runner. Finally, in 1989, the Apple II launched seminal fantasy platform game Prince of Persia, which represented a great leap forward in the quality of animation seen in video games.

However, the arrival of wealth and fame had an unexpected consequence. In February 1981, Wozniak was injured after crashing his Beechcraft Bonanza while taking off from a local airport. This accident had a profound impact on Wozniak's future at the company. He eventually returned to Apple product development in 1983 but his ambitions had changed dramatically and he wanted no more than a role of an engineer.

By now, Apple and Jobs had turned their attention to a small research effort called Macintosh, producing a computer with a graphics-rich interface and a mouse that allowed users to navigate much more easily than they could with keyboard commands.

The Mac was launched with one of the most famous TV commercials in history, titled 1984, and given a single showing during the Super Bowl of January that year. It associated IBM, at the time the major force in personal computers, with the Big Brother of George Orwell's Nineteen Eighty-Four.

Bill Gates, chairman of Microsoft, appeared on stage with Jobs at the Mac's launch, praising the machine and promising Microsoft's software support. Unfortunately, after an initial burst, the Mac failed to sell in the expected quantities.

In 1985, Apple closed half its six factories, shed 1,200 employees (a fifth of its staff) and declared its first quarterly loss. Jobs lost a boardroom battle against John Sculley – the man he had hired from Pepsi as chief executive officer.

Jobs set up a new company, NeXT, to produce a powerful, futuristic Unix workstation for business and higher education users, taking several Apple employees, including members of the Mac team. Technologists took to the computers

BELOW Bill Gates

— including British computer scientist Tim Berners-Lee, who used them to create the World Wide Web in the early 1990s. But at $6,000, they were too expensive for consumers and failed to catch on.

However, this setback didn't hit Jobs as hard as it would have done many others. By now Jobs was the consummate performer. When he launched the NeXT in the UK from the illustrious setting of the stage of the iconic London Palladium he was by now a sublimely polished orator. He had also begun to dabble in moviemaking technology, and in 1986 bought a small computer graphics division from filmmaker George Lucas' Lucasfilm Ltd. and renamed it Pixar.

He had also met Laurene Powell, a Stanford business student, and they were married in 1991 by a Buddhist monk. Plus he had been reunited with his biological mother, Joanne Simpson, and biological sister, Mona Simpson. He and his sister became close, and she dedicated her 1992 novel Anywhere But Here to him and their mother.

Then, his life took an even greater about turn. In 1995, Pixar released the first feature-length computer-animated film Toy Story, which became a massive hit. The company went public one week later, making Jobs a billionaire.

His triumph at Pixar reminded people of his ability to perceive the technological future, and in 1997 he persuaded Apple to buy NeXT – to acquire its forward-looking operating system Nextstep, and, more importantly, Jobs himself. He was back at the company he had set up, and what he encountered was an organisation where the corporate atmosphere didn't reflect that of a thrusting business in a highly competitive market.

However, Jobs's instinctive feel for what the public wanted soon turned things around. Within a year the company was once more posting handsome profits.

The iMac computer was launched in 1998, followed in 2001 by the iPod, iTunes digital music software, and the iTunes online digital music Store. But it was in 2007, when Apple revealed the iPhone, an ingenious device that combined mobile phone, iPod, and internet device, closely followed by the iPad, a tablet device without a physical keyboard, when things changed forever in the video gaming industry.

The arrival of the iPhone and iPad represented a sea change. For years, Nintendo had enjoyed the majority of the handheld market all to itself. But when Apple created the App Store for its iPhone and opened it up to developers, you could get a quality game extremely cheaply, sometimes for free.

The likes of Angry Birds, Osmos, Plants vs. Zombies, Tiny Wings and Infinity Blade began to dominate the industry and they were the perfect complement for the iPad. In fact, the sheer variety and number of games that Apple made available transformed the world of gaming. Jobs had pulled off the impossible once more and confounded his sceptics. In little more than a decade, he had taken Apple from near-bankruptcy to being the world's second most valuable company by market capitalisation, after the oil giant Exxon, with around $80bn in the bank.

Jobs wasn't exactly the perfect boss, though. He was renowned for his impatience for weakness, arrogance and ability to launch blistering tirades that left subordinates fuming, or in tears. He was also not afraid to blast rivals, specifically software giant Microsoft, whose products he once described as "really third-rate" and aesthetically tasteless.

But his mercurial brilliance, unparalleled touch with the changes in technology trends and incredible willpower set him aside from almost anyone else involved in the history of computers and gaming.

Sadly, after many years battling ill health, Jobs died of pancreatic cancer in 2011. His loss to the industry he had helped to build to stratospheric levels was immense.

As for the far more modest Wozniak, on the other hand, after leaving Apple in 1987, remained a shareholder employee of the company and received an annual stipend. He also maintained connections with Steve Jobs until his death but it was clear any close friendship they once shared had long gone. His disappointment at discovering his old friend's deception back in the mid 1970s was too great.

Chapter 7

Video and Computer Game History Timeline

1947

The earliest known interactive electronic game is developed by Thomas T. Goldsmith Jr. and Estle Ray Mann on a cathode ray tube. The game is a missile simulator inspired by radar displays from the Second World War which uses analogue circuitry, not digital, to control the CRT beam and position a dot on the screen. Screen overlays were used for targets since graphics could not be drawn at the time

1948

British mathematicians Alan Turing develop a computer chess program as an example of machine intelligence.

1951

The NIMROD computer, created by Ferranti, is presented during the Festival of Britain. Designed exclusively to play the game of NIM, this was the first instance of a digital computer designed specifically to play a game.

TV engineer Ralph Baer is asked to build "the best television set in the world" and comes up with the idea for playing games on the television set, but the idea was turned down.

Alan Turing's colleague Dr. Dietrich

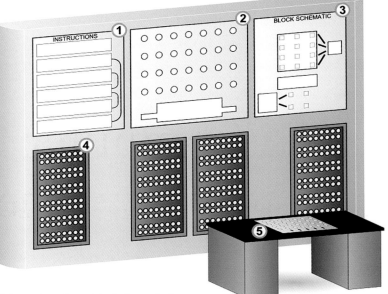

1. Instructions panel: instructions that Nimrod follows during the game

2. Main panel: bulbs mirror the control panel (5) to show the process of the game to the observers; underneath the bulbs there is a legend describing the possible states of the game.

3. Panel shows the current calculations of the processor during slow game speed; a legend for this is located on panel (1)

4. Four bays holding the machine's valves (tubes). Each bay contains 120 valves, arranged as six blocks of twenty. (Only 350 of the installed valves were active in the computer; the others were just being 'burned in' to avoid early failure.)

5. Nimrod's control panel: demonstrator would typically sit on the side closer to the computer, while the player would sit on the other side of the desk.

Prinz writes the original chess-playing program for Manchester University's Ferranti computer.

1952

OXO (also known as Noughts and Crosses) is written for the EDSAC computer by Alexander Douglas.

1958

American physicist Willy Higinbotham invents Tennis for Two, an interactive table tennis-like game that is displayed on an oscilloscope.

1961

MIT students create Spacewar!. Programmed by Steve Russell, Spacewar! is the first interactive computer game.

1964

Rosen Enterprises, started by David Rosen and now Japan's largest amusement company, merges with Service Games to form Sega enterprises.

1966

Ralph Baer starts to research interactive television games at Sanders Associates.

Sega releases Periscope, which is so successful in Japan it becomes the country's first amusement export.

1968

Ralph Baer patents his first interactive television game.

1969

Nolan Bushnell graduates from the University of Utah and accepts a job in California.

BELOW Magnavox ODYSSEY 200 console

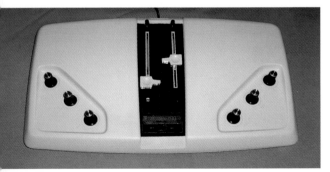

1970

Magnavox licenses Ralph Baer's television game from Sanders Associates.

Bushnell begins work on an arcade version of Spacewar! called Computer Space.

1971

Bill Pitts and Hugh Tuck develop the first coin-operated computer game, Galaxy Game, at Stanford University

Two months after Galaxy Game's installation, Computer Space is released, becoming the first coin-operated video game to be commercially sold (and the first widely available video game of any kind).

Both games were variations on Spacewar!, but Computer Space used an actual video display by having an actual television set in the cabinet.

1972

Magnavox begins demonstrating Odyssey in private showings, one of which is attended by Bushnell. He leaves Nutting and starts Syzygy with partner Ted Dabney. After discovering the name is already taken, they rename their company Atari.

Atari engineers Al Alcorn creates Pong.

Magnavox releases Odyssey. It then sues Atari on the grounds that Pong infringes on Baer's patents. Bushnell opts to settle out of court.

1973

Midway, Taito, and Williams enter the video game business.

1975

Atari creates the Home Pong unit and sells the idea to Sears Roebuck.

Namco begins making video games.

Midway Games imports Gunfight, a Taito game, the first game to use a microprocessor.

1976

Fairchild Camera & Instruments releases

ABOVE Apple Lisa

Channel F, the first programmable home game console to use cartridges.
Bushnell sells Atari to Warner Communications for $28 million.

The first Apple computer is released. Only around 200 were made.

1977

The second Apple Computer is released, part of the first wave of mass-produced home computers.

Atari releases the Video Computer System (VCS), later renamed the Atari 2600.

Bally releases the Bally Professional Arcade home console.

Shigeru Miyamoto joins Nintendo, which also releases its first home video game in Japan.

1978

Bushnell is forced out of Atari and Ray Kassar becomes the company's CEO.

Nintendo releases its first arcade game, Othello.

Midway releases Space Invaders.

Magnavox releases the Odyssey[2].

Cinematronics releases Space Wars, an arcade adaptation of Spacewars

1979

Capcom is founded in Japan.

Atari releases Asteroids, the company's all-time bestselling game.

Warren Robinett, Atari game designer, introduces the concept of Easter Eggs to

video games by hiding a room with his name in Adventure.

The first handheld programmable game system, called Microvision, is released by Milton Bradley.

1980

Atari releases Space Invaders for the VCS, launching the concept of selling home versions of arcade hits.

Activision is created.
Namco releases the landmark Pac-Man, the most popular arcade game of all time.

1981

IBM's PC (personal computer) is released.

Nintendo releases Donkey Kong.

Atari releases Pac-Man for the VCS.

US arcades' revenues reach $5 billion.

Electronic Games, the first magazine dedicated to the video game industry is published.

1982

Commodore releases the Commodore 64, the best-selling home computer model of all-time.

The ZX Spectrum is released. It would become the UK's leading home computer during the mid 1980s.
Atari releases the 5200 game console.

Midway releases Mc Pac-Man, which would become the most successful American-produced arcade game.

1983

Sega releases its first home console in Japan – SG-1000.

1984

Nintendo releases the Famicom (the Family Computer) in Japan.

Warner Communications sells Atari Corporation to Commodore Computers founder Jack Tramiel but retains the arcade division as Atari Games.

Apple releases the Macintosh, the first personal computer with a graphical user interface.

1985

Nintendo tests the Famicom in New York as the NES (Nintendo Entertainment System).

BELOW NES Console

Russian mathematician Alex Pajitnov designs Tetris.

Platform classic Super Mario Bros. is released.

1986

The NES is released nationwide.

Sega releases the Sega master System.

Atari releases the 7800 game console.

1987

The Legend of Zelda and Mike Tyson's Punch-Out!! are released by Nintendo.

Sega unveils 16-bit Mega Drive game console.

Final Fantasy is released in Japan.

1988

Tonka acquires the US distribution rights to the Sega Master System.

1989

Sega releases the Mega Drive as Genesis in the United States.

Nintendo releases the Game Boy world-wide.

Fantasy platform game Prince of Persia is released for the Apple II. The game represented a great leap forward in the quality of video game animation.

1990

Nintendo releases Super Mario Bros. 3 – the most successful non-bundled game cartridge of all time.

1991

Nintendo of America releases Super NES.

Sega unveils both its new game and

BELOW Sega Genesis Mod2

mascot – Sonic The Hedgehog.

Capcom releases Street Fighter II.

1992

Sega takes control of the US console market.

Sonic The Hedgehog II is released.

1993

Broderbund publishes Myst for Macintosh Computers. Meanwhile, Id Software publishes Doom for PCs.

1994

The Interactive Digital Software Association is created in response to Senate hearings on video game violence.

Nintendo releases Donkey Kong Country and retakes control of the US console market.

Sega releases Sonic The Hedgehog III. It then releases Saturn in Japan.

Sony releases PlayStation in Japan.

ABOVE N64 Console

1995

Sega releases Saturn in the US.

Sony releases PlayStation in the US.

Nintendo unveils the 64-bit Nintendo 64 game console in Japan.

1996

The Nintendo 64 is released in the US. The company also sells its billionth cartridge worldwide.

Sony unveils Crash Bandicoot.

Notable for its female protagonist, one of the biggest-selling video games franchises of all-time, Tomb Raider, begins.

1997

DMA Design (now Rockstar North) creates Grand Theft Auto, which is made available on PlayStation, CD-ROM, Game Boy Color and to download.

Saturn is discontinued by Sega.

Bandai releases Tamagotchi, the portable virtual pet.

Dreamworks, Universal, and Sega join forces to form a new line of super arcades called GameWorks.

Nintendo releases GoldenEye 007 for Nintendo 64.

PlayStation unveil Final Fantasy VII.

1998

Nintendo's Pokémon arrives in America and starts a new craze.

1999

Hasbro buys Atari from JTS.

Sega releases the Dreamcast console.

2000

Sony releases PlayStation 2, first in Japan and then later in the year in America.

Microsoft unveils plans for the Xbox video game console.

2001

Sega discontinues Dreamcast.

Nintendo releases GameCube in the US.

Microsoft releases Xbox worldwide with Halo: Combat Evolved as its exclusive launch title.

2003

The PlayStation 3 is released.

Activision's first-person shooter video game Call of Duty is released. It would go on to spawn several extremely popular sequels.

2004

Nintendo's DS handheld console is

released, boasting a dual screen, wireless multi-player gaming and a stylus for interacting with its touch screen.

2005

Microsoft's second games console, the Xbox 360 is released.

Guitar Hero is released on PlayStation 2. The game features a guitar-shaped controller that the player uses to simulate playing rock music

2006

The motion-based Wii is released.

2007

Apple releases the touchscreen iPhone smartphone, capable of playing thousands of downloadable games.

The first in the historical action adventure series Assassin's Creed is released on Xbox and 360 and PlayStation 3.

2009

Angry Birds is released for Apple's iOS.

Its success first prompted Apple to design versions for other smartphones and then expand to video game consoles and PCs.

2010

Microsoft's Kinect is released, enabling users to control and interact with the Xbox 360 using gestures and spoken commands. A version for Windows was released in 2012.

2012

The Wii's successor, the Wii U, is released – the first entry in the eighth generation of video game home consoles, the current iteration.

2013

A rebooted Tomb Raider is unveiled.

ABOVE Xbox 360 Console

Chapter 8

The Eight Generations (And Rising) Of Video Consoles

The video game may take the glory but each and every game is tied to a particular piece of hardware and since Ralph Baer's Magnavox Odyssey was released in 1972, the world has also fallen in love with the games console.

RIGHT Odyssey 200

FIRST GENERATION

By the autumn of 1975, Magnavox, bowing to the popularity of Pong, cancelled the Odyssey and released a scaled-down version, the Odyssey 100. A second, "higher end" console, the Odyssey 200, was released with the 100 and added onscreen scoring, up to four players, and a third game to go with Tennis and Hockey - Smash.

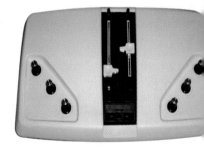

At the same time Atari released their own home Pong console and it was these consoles that jump-started the consumer market.

This initial period of video game console technology was termed the first generation and since those heady early days eight generations of consoles have so far come to pass.

SECOND GENERATION

The second generation of computer and video games (sometimes referred to as the early 8-bit era) began in 1976 with the release of the Fairchild Video Entertainment System (VES). The early period of this generation saw the release of several consoles as various companies decided to enter the market; later, the releases were in direct response to the earlier consoles.

The VES was the first console to use microprocessor-based hardware and ROM cartridges containing game code, instead of having non microprocessor dedicated hardware with all games built in.

However, it was the release of the incredibly successful Atari 2600 (originally called the Atari VCS) in 1977 that made the plug-in concept popular among the game-playing public. Atari

had also secured a deal with Sears to sell the console through its department stores, this clever move sealed its status as the dominant console for much of the second generation.

In 2009, the Atari 2600 was named the second greatest video game console of all time by IGN, who cited its remark-

BELOW Fairchild Channel F

able role as the console behind both the first video game boom and called it "the console that our entire industry is built upon".

ABOVE Atari 2600
Wood 4Sw

soles, leaving only Atari and Magnavox standing in the home console market. Their survival came at a heavy cost, though, as both companies suffered massive losses in 1977 and 1978.

THIRD GENERATION

It was not until Atari released their conversion of the gigantic arcade hit Space Invaders in 1980 that the home console industry was completely revived. Space Invaders' unprecedented success started the trend of console manufacturers trying to get exclusive rights to arcade titles, and the trend of advertisements for game consoles claiming to bring the arcade experience home.

The release of Atari's VCS also convinced Fairchild to rename the VES as Channel F. By the end of 1977 it had sold 250,000 consoles, second only to the VCS. However, other consoles such as the Mattel Intellivision, the Magnavox Odyssey2, and ColecoVision also enjoying market share.

The Fall and Rise of the Games Console
The year after the release of the VES, manufacturers of older, obsolete consoles and Pong clones sold their systems at a loss to clear stock, creating a glut in the market. As a result Fairchild and RCA had to abandon their game con-

As the 1980s rolled on, several other companies released video game consoles of their own, many of which were technically superior to the Atari 2600. Despite this, the public continued to place their trust in Atari and the company dominated the console market in the early part of the decade.

In 1982, another version of the Atari VCS four-switch console was released, this time without wood grain. The machines were nicknamed "Darth Vader" consoles due to their distinctive all-black appearance and were the first consoles to be officially called "Atari 2600", as the Atari 5200 was released the same year.

However, the same year as the release of Atari's "Darth Vader" console, a glut of mediocre games from a host of new games publishers were released, flooding the market. Most stores had insufficient space to carry new games and consoles and when they tried to return the surplus games to the new publishers, the publishers had neither new products nor cash to issue refunds to the retailers. Consequently, the industry suffered its second crash in 1983, and this time no one was safe.

The worst hit of the consoles was the Atari 2600, whose rushed Pac-Man game was a massive letdown, but nowhere near as disappointing as its widely trumpeted E.T. game. The end result is widely considered to be one of the worst video games ever. Combined with the high costs for the movie license, E.T. became another financial failure for Atari and the company was sold two years later as the crash impacted upon the industry.

In America, video games were seen as a fad that had already passed and it looked like the games console had enjoyed the last of its glory days. But a saviour for the industry would arrive in the form of a diminutive Italian plumber.

Nintendo brought their Japanese Family Computer (the Famicom as it was known in Japan) over to America in 1985 and rebranded it as the Nintendo Entertainment System (NES). The machine came packaged with the addictive gaming classic Super Mario Bros., and it inclusion with the NES ensured everyone wanted to get their hands on the console "that played Super Mario Bros.".

The success of the NES revived the video game industry and ushered in a new third generation, and before long, new consoles were soon introduced to compete with the NES. One such console was Sega's Master System, which, unfortunately for Sega, didn't manage to secure any significant market share in America and was barely profitable.

FOURTH GENERATION

More commonly referred to as the 16-bit era, the fourth generation of games consoles began on October 30, 1987 with the Japanese release of NEC's PC Engine (known as the TurboGrafx-16 in North America).

However, although NEC released the first fourth generation console, this era saw a continuation of the rivalry between Nintendo and Sega. Their respective consoles – the Super Nintendo Entertainment System (the Super Famicom in Japan) and the Mega Drive (named the Sega Genesis in North America due to trademark

BELOW Sega Genesis Model2 32X

issues) – were released, and this time Sega had an ace up its sleeve, in the form of a speedy hedgehog.

Sonic The Hedgehog, released in 1991, proved to be the breakout hit Sega craved and soon they were extending the Mega Drive with the Sega Mega-CD (known simply as the Sega CD in North America), to provide increased storage space for multimedia-based games that were then in vogue among the development community.

Later, Sega released the 32X, which added some of the polygon-processing functionality common in fifth-generation machines. However, the peripheral was a commercial failure due to a lack of software support.

As the 1990s rolled on, it became clear that this was a decade of marked innovation in video gaming, marking a transition from raster graphics to 3D graphics. Plus, several genres of video games had emerged, including first-person shooter, real-time strategy, and MMO (massively multiplayer online games).

Handheld gaming began to become

Rodgers suggested the family orientated, Alexey Pajitnov-designed Tetris as an alternative, Nintendo was convinced.

LEFT Nintendo Gameboy

Tetris proved crucial to the massive success of the handheld, with more than 40 million Game Boys with copies of Tetris sold worldwide. It let Nintendo secure a level of dominance in the handheld games market that was even greater than its hold on the games console business.

However, arcade games, although still relatively popular in the early 1990s, begin a decline as home consoles become more common.

more popular throughout the decade, thanks in part to the release of the Game Boy in 1989. The Game Boy was the latest invention of Gunpei Yokoi, the Nintendo engineer who designed the company's Game & Watch line of handheld games.

FIFTH GENERATION

Eschewing the flashy gimmicks of the Atari Lynx and Sega's Game Gear, the Game Boy's selling points were its unrivalled 10-hour battery life and lower retail price. Nintendo had planned on making Super Mario Land the lead game for the machine, but when an American entrepreneur called Henk

The first fifth-generation consoles were the 3DO and the Atari Jaguar, both much more powerful than the SNES or Mega Drive. However, neither of these consoles were serious threats to Sega or Nintendo as the 3DO cost more than the SNES and Genesis combined, and the Jaguar was extremely difficult to program for. Their time in the market proved short-lived and both consoles were discontinued in 1996.

ABOVE Atari Jaguar

It was not until Sega's Saturn, Sony's PlayStation, and the Nintendo 64 were released that fifth generation consoles started to become popular. The standout in this successful trio was the PlayStation.

Released in Japan in December 1994 and America and Europe the following year, the PlayStation was the first entry in a console franchise that has become something of a leviathan. With addictive classics such as Crash Bandicoot, the PlayStation was the first video game system to sell more 100 million consoles. Ultimately, the PlayStation and

Nintendo 64 had crushed Sega's Saturn console, leaving the company nursing a multi-million dollar loss. But Sega already had their riposte to this failure up its sleeve. Their next console would usher in the next generation of consoles and up the ante in Sega's fascinating battle with Sony and Nintendo.

SIXTH GENERATION

And so, as gaming headed towards the next century, Sega's Dreamcast was unveiled to the world in November 1998. It would prove to be both a creative high point and a commercial nadir for the company.

For all of Sega's ambition and creativity, the company's efforts to convince the world to own its groundbreaking new console failed. When Sony released its PlayStation 2 in March 2000, sales of the Dreamcast sunk dramatically.

In January 2001, Sega stopped production of the Dreamcast completely and made the bold step of reinventing itself as a publisher of games for the consoles made by its former rivals. It felt like the end of an era.

The PlayStation 2 went on to not only wipe out Sega, but it also utterly eclipsed Nintendo's rival Gamecube console; plus, to add to the pressure, Microsoft had just thrown its hat into the console business ring with its Xbox. Until the Xbox, Microsoft had sat on the sidelines of the video game business, but the Xbox changed all that.

ABOVE Xbox Console

Backed by its flagship first-person shooter Halo: Combat Evolved, the Xbox became the first American-made games console to gain a significant share of the market since Atari's 2600 in the early 1980s. Monopolising the American and European market, Microsoft managed to sell 24 million Xboxes, compared to the 22 million Gamecubes sold by Nintendo.

Nintendo's defeat saw the company rethink its approach to console and game design. They decided to surprise everyone and in November 2004 unveiled its first attempt at a new concept all together: the Nintendo DS, a handheld console that boasted two screens, one a touch screen that players interacted with using a stylus.

Its multi-generational charm appealed to younger players with games such as virtual pet game Nintendogs, while puzzle game Dr Kawashima's Brain Training captured the attention of the older audience.

SEVENTH GENERATION

Microsoft kicked off the seventh generation with the release of the Xbox 360 console in late 2005 in America, Europe and Japan, and then March 2006 in Australia.

The Xbox boasted high-definition graphics, a larger hard drive and more support for online multiplayer games. The console performed well, but it was the release of Nintendo's Wii in

November 2006 that made the video game industry face up to the new wave of technological innovation.

Nintendo had been trying to reinvent the video game controller since it began developing its Nintendo 64 console in 1996. The company believed, rightly, that the latest graphical breakthroughs were no longer impressing players and

BELOW Nintendo Wii Console

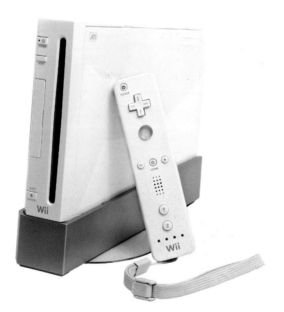

so a new wow factor was needed. As a result, Nintendo created a simplified game controller designed to look like a TV remote control that allowed players to play simply by moving the remote around. The Wii was born.

On the back of this clever breakthrough and complemented by the infectious gameplay of Wii Sports, the Wii's flagship launch game, by late 2009 Nintendo had sold nearly 70 million Wiis. Microsoft's Xbox 360 and Sony's PlayStation 3 had both sold half that amount.

Nintendo's decision to break from the pack had paid massive dividends. They were top of the video game tree once more. As a result, Sony and Microsoft started to develop motion controllers of their own.

EIGHTH GENERATION

Here's to the Future...

More than fifty years have elapsed since the creators of Spacewar! became the first people to truly experience what a video game was. Since then, the games console is a product that has evolved over four decades into something that has won a place in millions of living rooms.

The Wii U was released in late 2012 and its arrival saw the birth of the eighth, and, some believe, potentially the last, generation of the home video game console. Its arrival cemented the video games console's position at the heart of an entertainment industry that rivals Hollywood. But where does it go next? Today, more people of all ages are playing games than ever before, but they're finding different and cheaper ways of playing, especially on smart phones and tablet computers. That could spell trouble for the console.

According to Sony, the PlayStation 4 is the future of gaming. The first PlayStation, released in 1994, racked up more than 100 million sales; in 2000 the PS2 did even better, selling 155 million. However, the PlayStation 3 – which has faced stiffer competition since its 2006 launch – has sold just over 70 million. Is this a telling statistic?

Sony and its rivals are betting that the console will have a new future as an all-purpose entertainment device. However, making money from gaming keeps getting harder. Only time will tell.

One thing is for sure, the video game remains an art form that feels like it has barely started. The insatiable appetite of gamers around the globe and the unwavering ambition of leading game designers mean video games stand on the crest of a new era of creativity.

Video games, once thought to be a fad, have worked their way into the fabric of international culture, and with every successive generation, the video game industry just keeps growing. In short, the game never ends. Long may it continue.

BELOW Wii U Console and Gamepad

The pictures in this book were provided courtesy of the following:

WIKIMEDIA COMMONS

Design & Artwork: ALEX YOUNG

Published by: DEMAND MEDIA LIMITED & G2 ENTERTAINMENT LIMITED

Publishers: JASON FENWICK & JULES GAMMOND

Written by: ANDREW O'BRIEN